Do No Harm?

Munchausen Syndrome by Proxy

Craig McGill

First published in Great Britain by Vision Paperbacks, a division of Satin Publications Ltd.

Vision Paperbacks
101 Southwark Street
London SE1 0JH
UK
e-mail: info@visionpaperbacks.co.uk
website: www.visionpaperbacks.co.uk

Publisher: Sheena Dewan
Cover design © 2002 Nickolai Globe
Typeset by FiSH Books, London WC1
Printed and bound in the UK by Cromwell Press

ISBN: 1-901250-48-2

Contents

Author's Note

In the chapters that are real-life stories, the names of people and places involved have been altered. In some cases this is at the request of the people involved; in others it is for legal reasons. Some places have also been left unidentified, again for legal reasons.

No names in the other chapters have been altered, unless stated.

Acknowledgements

An emotive topic like this one, shrouded in secrecy, is a gruelling task for anyone and I was fortunate that a lot of people were there to help me stay focused.

Anyone who spoke to me or helped with comments for this book, regardless of their opinion on MSBP, is thanked. Many cannot be named for legal reasons or have chosen to stay anonymous. These people, and those who are named in the book, have my gratitude as well as my admiration for being so strong.

At Vision, thanks to Sheena Dewan and Stella Wood for backing the idea that MSBP should no longer be a topic that seemed to be hidden from the mainstream of society.

As the tone of the book indicates, this was not a cheerful book to write and I burdened more than one friend with my doubts over being able to do the people involved justice. They gave me not only the confidence to carry on, but also cheered me up when needed – sometimes until the wee small hours. So thanks to Deborah Lee, Stephen McPartlin, Sharon Henderson, Pamela Fraser, David Henderson and his Newcastle colleagues, Ron Moore, Michael Tierney, Shaun Milne, Caroline Miller, Bill MacDonald, Julie Burke, Clare Crerar, Gillian Kernohan, Tamzin Lewis and Catherine and Jaqueline Ferns, as well as many others.

On the journalism side I'd like to thank some of my previous editors – Bill Allsopp, Neil McIntosh, Harry Roulston and Tom Christie – for not only giving me a break when it was needed but also for teaching me some of the essential values of digging for stories and reminding me that a story without heart is not a story, just a collection of words.

Thanks also to Penny, Brian, Tamie and others for their work over the years in trying to bring MSBP into the public forum.

Special thanks also go to Dougie Watson for knowing what it's all about. Thanks also to senior staff at the *Press and Journal* and the *Sunday Mirror*, the Fleet Street lists on the Internet and the Association of Investigative Journalists.

Special mention also has to go to Marie McFadyen, Mary Burns and Isobel Watson for being part-time mums in looking after this boy from Carntyne. None of them are related to me, but they always treated me just like family and for that they will always have my love.

And thanks, with love, to my own mother, Ann, who could never have been accused of MSBP.

Lastly, Karen. Much love. Today, all our tomorrows and all the yesterdays. Always.

Craig McGill
Scotland
November 2001

Hippocratic Oath – Classical

I swear by Apollo the Physician and Asclepius and Hygieia and Panaceia and all the gods and goddesses, making them my witnesses, that I will fulfil according to my ability and judgement this oath and this covenant:

To hold him who has taught me this art as equal to my parents and to live my life in partnership with him, and if he is in need of money to give him a share of mine, and to regard his offspring as equal to my brothers in male lineage and to teach them this art – if they desire to learn it – without fee and covenant; to give a share of precepts and oral instruction and all the other learning to my sons and to the sons of him who has instructed me and to pupils who have signed the covenant and have taken an oath according to the medical law, but no one else.

I will apply dietetic measures for the benefit of the sick according to my ability and judgement; I will keep them from harm and injustice.

I will neither give a deadly drug to anybody who asked for it, nor will I make a suggestion to this effect. Similarly I will not give to a woman an abortive remedy. In purity and holiness I will guard my life and my art.

I will not use the knife, not even on sufferers from stone, but will withdraw in favour of such men as are engaged in this work.

Whatever houses I may visit, I will come for the benefit of the sick, remaining free of all intentional injustice, of all mischief and in particular of sexual relations with both female and male persons, be they free or slaves.

What I may see or hear in the course of the treatment or even outside of the treatment in regard to the life of men, which on no account one must spread abroad, I will keep to myself, holding such things shameful to be spoken about.

If I fulfil this oath and do not violate it, may it be granted to me to enjoy life and art, being honoured with fame among all men for all time to come; if I transgress it and swear falsely, may the opposite of all this be my lot.

Translated from the Greek by Ludwig Edelstein. From *The Hippocratic Oath: Text, Translation and Interpretation* (1943) Ludwig Edelstein, Johns Hopkins Press, Baltimore.

Hippocratic Oath – Modern

I swear to fulfil, to the best of my ability and judgement, this covenant:

I will respect the hard-won scientific gains of those physicians in whose steps I walk, and gladly share such knowledge as is mine with those who are to follow.

I will apply, for the benefit of the sick, all measures which are required, avoiding those twin traps of overtreatment and therapeutic nihilism.

I will remember that there is art to medicine as well as science, and that warmth, sympathy and understanding may outweigh the surgeon's knife or the chemist's drug.

I will not be ashamed to say 'I know not', nor will I fail to call in my colleagues when the skills of another are needed for a patient's recovery.

I will respect the privacy of my patients, for their problems are not disclosed to me that the world may know. Most especially must I tread with care in matters of life and death. If it is given me to save a life, all thanks. But it may also be within my power to take a life; this awesome responsibility must be faced with great humbleness and awareness of my own frailty. Above all, I must not play at God.

I will remember that I do not treat a fever chart, a cancerous growth, but a sick human being, whose illness may affect the person's family and economic stability. My responsibility includes these related problems, if I am to care adequately for the sick.

I will prevent disease whenever I can, for prevention is preferable to cure.

I will remember that I remain a member of society, with special obligations to all my fellow human beings, those sound of mind and body as well as the infirm.

If I do not violate this oath, may I enjoy life and art, respected while I live and remembered with affection thereafter. May I always act so as to preserve the finest traditions of my calling and may I long experience the joy of healing those who seek my help.

Written in 1964 by Louis Lasagna, Academic Dean of the School of Medicine at Tufts University, and used in many medical schools worldwide today.

Introduction

'What would you know about being a mother and having your child taken away, you're a male with no kids!'

When people heard I was writing a book about Munchausen Syndrome by Proxy (which, for the sake of brevity, will be referred to as MSBP for the rest of the book) that was a common question asked. It's not what you would call a trendy topic that a lot of people are talking about; it's something that appears in the press very irregularly and has been used as the 'bizarre medical symptom of the week' on TV programmes like *Casualty* and *E.R.*

So what is MSBP and why is there the need for this book?

MSBP is a so-called condition where parents or people in charge of children – normally females – are accused of harming children; their own or others. It may be as simple as marking a baby by bruising or claiming they have breathing problems – or it could be more sinister, for example by poisoning their food.

In the UK, the most famous case of MSBP to date has been Beverley Allitt, the nurse who was jailed for life for murdering four children and attacking nine others, while in North America Kathy Bush, who met the First Lady and was a national celebrity, was accused of harming her own daughter, making her have more than 40 operations. However, the condition is treated as a freak syndrome, with little in-depth analysis. It's merely something that pops up from time to time.

If MSBP's so rare then, why write a book about it?

First, the accusations of the condition are not as rare as one would like to think – indeed more and more people are being accused of it every year. Any medical condition on the increase deserves to be looked at seriously and not just in the jargon-heavy specialist medical and psychiatric journals.

Second, as I discovered when working on the MSBP case that got me involved in the topic (a case that cannot be mentioned until at least 2010, so I cannot say any more about it. Suffice it to say I discovered the draconian laws involved and was repulsed, as any decent human being should be), the parents have little of the recourse that we expect people to have in the supposedly civilised 21st century. Their children are taken away and they have no public forum to call to account those who have done this. The parents are accused but they themselves cannot accuse their accusers. There is a Latin phrase that's appropriate here: *Quis custodiet custodes ipsos? –* Who will guard the guards themselves?

To have no recourse in this day and age – when we can put men on the moon and send letters across the world in a heartbeat thanks to the Internet – is not just wrong, it is grossly offensive to all concepts of freedom and human rights.

The cries of people accused of MSBP have been silenced. Britain's legal system – never the most open – prevents the accused from speaking to the public. Court orders, said to protect the children, do much more than that. They allow one side to dictate what is said and where it is said. The accused have no voice and no public representation through the press. And if no one knows they exist, how can people get involved to help? *Do No Harm?* does not seek to say whether there is a condition or not. I have my opinion but it is only an opinion and it is presented at the end. For the rest of this book I have used my journalistic training to remain neutral. This book is for both sides to present their arguments, for and against, good and bad. The only person who can tell you what you think about this is you. Not the state, not the mothers, not me. *Do No Harm?* has been written to inform, not to preach.

If you still aren't convinced, think of it this way:

You grow up, you get married, you have kids and you cry at

their weddings. That's meant to be the life for most mothers. Worries about their children's first day at school, their first cold, their first date.

Not any more.

In the last few decades, more and more women have found themselves accused of what many would say is the unthinkable – harming a child. Their own child.

For a growing number of women, the fairytale moments of baby's first steps, the first fall, the first kiss on a small cut that has them sobbing, are being replaced by the nightmare accusation of causing the tears and sobs.

It's on the increase and it could be happening next door to you, as these women have no protection from the State's accusations. No one to shield them from the accusations and whispering campaigns of being a bad mother.

'But these people are crazy', you say, but who has decided that for them and us? Are the experts that expert? Some would say they are only human like the rest of us and could make mistakes.

Regardless of whether or not these people are crazy, they should be able to state their case in public and then let others decide. They should not have their voices – their lives – locked away, only to be subject to rumour and the innuendo of being a bad parent, being talked about behind their backs.

Do you really know what people think of you as a parent?

Read this book and take a loving look at your child. It may be your last. Don't think it could never happen to you. That's what many of these people thought.

You could be next.

One

Mary, England

Engand. A country where every man has the right to make his home a castle, it is claimed. A country made famous for coming up with a state-run health service, ensuring free health care for all, regardless of class, age or income. Its doctors are said to be among the best in the world, but at the end of the day they are only human and as the poet Alexander Pope reminded us, to be human is to err.

Everyone makes mistakes, but the mistakes of doctors led to Mary Donaldson from just outside Yorkshire mistrusting them, and that mistrust may have led to her daughter becoming brain damaged.

And Mary cannot forgive. She cannot forgive the doctors who put her in that position, but most of all she cannot forgive herself.

The problems started in 1990, when her youngest daughter Joanne, then aged eight, was diagnosed with a hip disorder, which required medical treatment. The doctor wanted Joanne to be treated once a week for a few hours to see if that made a difference, but Mary was not satisfied that this was the best course of action and disagreed with her doctor, who had only recently started at the family's health centre.

According to Mary: 'The doctor wanted her to go through a course of treatment which I felt was not going to see my daughter cured or helped in any significant way and I demanded something more intensive, which I knew was available.

'I wanted the best treatment for her so she could have a normal, happy childhood.'

Joanne can still remember some of those early days, but not with the fond memories that most people have of their childhood.

'I was always getting stabbing pains in my right knee, or at least that's where the problem felt to me. I was young and I probably wasn't explaining myself to them too well.

'We later found out that it was a condition called Perthes Syndrome, which is a disease of the hip where the ball in your hip is not as hard as normal bone and it deforms how your bone fits into the socket.

'It didn't really sink into me when they said they couldn't treat me because of my age. All I knew was that I was sore at times and other times I wasn't and I didn't want to be sore.

'But when they said they couldn't cure it, just help me, it didn't sink in as the young me thought it was the same thing, but I always remember mum being really upset over it all.

'She then started demanding that I get the best treatment, going to various hospitals and specialists. She would never accept an opinion that didn't fit in with hers.'

After much fighting and arguing, Mary got Joanne moved to other hospitals for treatment and according to Mary, 'I'm sure I pissed off more than a few people at hospitals and clinics as I was downright arrogant with some of them because I knew there was a more intensive treatment out there that could make a drastic difference to my daughter's life.

'Perhaps I was rude, but it was not personal. I was just trying to get the best for my daughter like any parent would.

'So we changed hospitals and the more intensive treatment was made available to Joanne for a while, but the doctors there told me that they did not think it would help as much as I had believed and that perhaps the best course would be to go along with my original doctor's recommendation.

'Eventually, and after seeking out further opinion – including my daughter's – I agreed with them.'

Joanne recalls being angry with her mum at the time. 'The constant treatment had me in a lot of pain because of the work involved. I improved at first but after a while I stopped improving and all I was getting was constant pain.

'At one point I remember asking mum why she was hurting me so much, as I was getting afraid of approaching the clinic where I was being treated.

'I think that made her see that it might not be working as well as she had hoped.'

For Mary, going back to the original doctor was not a pleasant experience.

'When we returned to the first doctor, it was hardly sweetness and light. I got the opinion that he felt I had harmed my daughter by what I had done. He never said it outright, but by some of the snide comments he made, I knew he was throwing the blame at me.

'Over the visits, he started asking us both more and more questions about things that were happening outside the health centre. His comments came to the fore when Joanne mentioned that I occasionally used a wheelchair with her.

'To him, this was holding her back. He said it was like giving someone with a fractured ankle a walking plaster but tying them down. He was of the opinion that I was being a hindrance to my own daughter. My counter argument was that I was using the wheelchair at times for her own safety, nothing else.

'The sort of times we would use it would be if we were going for long journeys or getting her to and from school. I don't deny I was worried about her. She was my daughter for God's sake.

'Needless to say, words were exchanged and I don't deny I said a lot to the doctor that I shouldn't have, calling into question his credibility, training and background. I did almost call him once to apologise, but I just felt as if he would ram the words back at me, so I didn't.'

Joanne also recalls parts of the meeting that would transform the family for ever.

'I don't remember much of it, I just remember mum crying, but she told me a few times over the years that she and the doctor had disagreed over the best course of action for me. The doctor at one point said he would report my mother as she had been doing all the wrong things for me and she asked how could she be reported for wanting the best treatment for her daughter?'

Joanne stayed in the wheelchair and was then referred for an operation. 'Eventually I was told that an operation would take place. I didn't know what surgery was and when I was told what it was I could only keep thinking of Dad cutting up the Sunday roast or pulling a drumstick off a chicken. It really scared me and I didn't want an operation at first, but eventually mum convinced me that it would be for the best.'

A few months later, Joanne had the operation. Some bone was taken out of her pelvis and put in her hip to try to make the socket a better fit. Unfortunately it did not take the pain away.

Joanne recalls: 'At first I thought I was fine, but that was probably the anaesthetic still being in my system. After a week the pain did start to return but it wasn't as sharp as before, now it was more like a dull ache, like a constant toothache. When I concentrated I could ignore it, but it took a lot of effort.'

As time went on, the doctors and Joanne realised that the pain was more pronounced when the leg was being exerted, so she was put back in a wheelchair. At first this was a welcome relief, but as time went on and the time spent in the chair increased, it became a prison.

'I hated it. Earlier it had been very occasional and that was fine, but now it was becoming constant – even when I was in the house.

'I knew people would laugh and treat me differently. As a child I found that people would bend over and talk to me for a while, but some people would just talk to whoever was pushing my chair and ignore me, talking about me as if I wasn't there, while all I could do was stare at their midriff.'

While being in a wheelchair helped alleviate the pain, Joanne told her mum that she did not want to spend the rest of her life 'looking at bellybuttons' and wanted out of the chair. This was during the summer of 1993 and Mary remembers her daughter being frustrated at remaining on the sidelines of life while her friends and two sisters played happily, more or less carefree in the sun.

But as Joanne was trying to come to terms with life in a wheelchair, there were other things happening that would have a devastating effect for years to come.

The doctor had referred Mary to the social services department of the local council for mismanaging Joanne's health care. He felt she was an unfit mother.

The first Mary knew of this was when she was informed that social workers would be coming to meet her. When she was told, she says she was stunned.

'When they turned up, I asked them why they were coming out – it had all been very coy over the phone and by letter to arrange the visit – and they told me I had been accused of having Munchausen Syndrome by Proxy.

'The only thing I could think of was Beverley Allitt. For a moment I actually believed they were accusing me of murdering someone and the first thought I had was "Who will take the children to America next summer?" as we had started to plan a trip there.

'I also laughed as they told me this. It was a nervous laugh, but it probably didn't make me look like a good parent in front of them.'

The social workers explained that they wanted to talk to the children, to their friends and other adults and build up a background profile, but the work would be confidential and discreet.

'They wouldn't tell me who had accused me of this, which really frightened me, as I thought anyone could accuse you.

'For a while I was comforted by the thought that perhaps this was nothing more than a malicious prank, but then I started to think that perhaps it had something to do with my insistence on Joanne getting the alternative treatment, which had turned out to be more painful. But that had been more than a year earlier and while I knew social services always have a backlog of work that struck me as too long back.

'It was only when I was asked about the wheelchair that I realised where this had all come from.'

Joanne remembers the first time someone asked about her mum.

'I was at school and someone asked me why my mum tortured me. I said she didn't and this other girl said it was going round the school that my mum broke my legs all the time to stop me running away.

'It wasn't until years later that I told my mum this, as mum was devastated at the time. I was petrified as kids kept telling me that I was going to be put in a home and my mum had always told me that only bad children went to homes, meaning care homes, which always seem foreboding and horrible places in children's books.

'I was always asking mum if I was a good child. She always told me yes, but one day, after I heard her and dad were splitting up, I was in tears, asking her if they were breaking up because I was a bad girl.

'I had it in my head that they were breaking up because of me and that I would be put in a home for being bad while they would each take one of my sisters and I'd never see any of them again.'

At the start of 1994 Mary and her husband Michael had realised that their marriage was no longer working. They had decided to stay in the same house for the sake of the children and were still cordial towards each other, but to both of them the marriage was over.

Michael is honest about what went wrong. 'It was a gradual case of realising that the two people we had been when we met were no longer the two people that we were and while we were still fond of each other and there was a love, it wasn't a love between man and wife.

'We both realised it at the same time, but we were worried about the effect this would have on the children, so it was decided that we would all stay together for a few years until the children were more grown up.

'This plan fell apart after a few months because a house nearby came up for rent. I went for it and lived there. I was near enough for the children to come and see me and vice versa.

'There were strains. Other partners could not understand the ease Mary and I still had with each other, but the biggest problems involved the kids.

'Not only did they keep trying to engineer ways of getting us back together, they started wetting the bed and sleeping badly, which did not look good when parents are being accused of being harmful to their children.'

The investigation into the family's behaviour took its toll in many ways. As well as the taunts Joanne endured, she also faced questioning from the social workers. Combined with what was already going through her head, she was unsure how to answer. She was worried that whatever was said, she would lose her mother.

'A few days into the investigation a social worker visited our house to ask me some questions about mum. He was nice and friendly, but he asked me a lot of awkward questions.

'He asked me if mum ever took me to the doctor's or hospital, even when I didn't feel ill or if she fussed over herself. I was also asked how her cooking tasted.

'I told the social worker over and over again that my mum loved me and would never hurt me, and he kept saying that he hadn't asked me if mum had ever hurt me. At times I felt as if he was trying to trick me. Looking back I'm sure he wasn't, but that was how I was looking at it then. I just didn't know what answer to give.

'Mum also had to attend lots of meetings to decide whether or not she'd been treating me properly. I knew they were just trying to make sure I was safe, but it was upsetting to know they were accusing my mum of hurting me and I was scared of what might happen to me next. With the taunting at school, I was worried about ending up in the so-called home.'

Family members were forbidden to talk to each other about anything involving the investigation. This tore Joanne apart, especially as she could see how it was affecting her mother.

'When we were in bed, I could hear her sobbing that she was afraid that they were going to take her babies away from her.

'Because of the abuse I was getting at school, and the stress at home, I was not the best of children and I started lashing out to try and get sympathy. Looking back, I was being a brat but then I just wanted everything to be normal again.

'I was sure mum wasn't trying to hurt me, but having all these adults telling me that something might be wrong made it hard to believe that there wasn't, especially as mum had always told us that adults tell the truth, so it was really hard to work out who was telling the truth and what was going on.'

Nine months after the letter had first dropped through the door, the social workers informed Mary and Michael that they did not believe there were any grounds for concern and added that the children were being brought up without harm and interference, but they were going through a hard time as puberty was about to kick in, combined with the divorce.

The children's names were never put on the council's 'at risk' register and Joanne never had to find out if there was a 'home' for bad children.

After the inquiry and clearing, Mary learned that the doctor she had argued with, which had led to the investigation, had accused other parents of MSBP, but Mary never discovered if any other parent accused was found to have it.

This left Mary relieved. The parents splitting up was an issue that would hopefully resolve itself over time. Michael was more worried about street gossip, as a number of people had already asked him what the social workers had been up to and the last thing he wanted or needed was for people to know that he, a policeman, was accused of being a bad parent.

'I was investigated and spoken to just like Mary, but they seemed to concentrate their work on finding out if she was a bad mother, instead of seeing if either of us were bad parents. I remember asking about MSBP and saying to them that if it was a mental condition then either of us could have it, not just Mary.

They acknowledged that, but said they had their reasons for working the way they did.

'Word did get out about it, but it was more about Mary being a bad mother. My job was never affected – I'm sure there were comments made behind my back, but there was never anything placed on my record, which had been a worry. It would turn out that we were worrying about the wrong record.'

And while the family are still bitter over their experiences, Joanne recognises one good thing that came out of it.

'We realised that as a family we loved and cared for each other. It does sound like a cliché, but we came through it. Even mum and dad realised that while they may not stay married, there was a bond between them.'

Mary found herself praising one particular group afterwards.

'I know they get a hard time, but in my experience the social work team were excellent. At the time it felt like going through Hell, but they were so thorough and dedicated that in the end they knew we were just like any other family. We were far from perfect, but the children were not being abused.

'But I did not come out of the situation with any respect for medical staff. I was already wary of them before the investigation, but after it I had no respect for them.

'Where possible I avoided the children having any contact with medical people that were not known to us as friends of the family.'

As Michael stated, the investigation was left on a report, but not his. When Mary and the children moved house, they had to change doctors and their new female doctor dropped a bombshell on Mary, a bombshell she will take to her grave.

'My new doctor was speaking to me and she mentioned that it stated on my file [that] I had been investigated for mental illness. I told her that wasn't the case and there was no history of mental illness in the family.

'Before she could say anything else though, the penny dropped. I asked her if it was MSBP. She said yes. I explained the background to her and then asked her to remove the details.

'She said she couldn't. She did not have the authority.'

Legal advice then added another blow.

'Lawyers told me that I can only remove the mention of the accusations if I take legal action through the civil courts. There are two problems with that. The first is that it is a very expensive and time-consuming exercise.

'Second, no one has ever succeeded in getting records changed in this way, so the allegations will stay on my notes for ever.

'This made me really angry and almost triggered depression. I couldn't believe that because of someone's accusations – which had been proven to be false – I was going to be tagged as having a mental illness all my days.'

Fast forward a few years. In 1997, three years after the divorce came through, Mary and Michael tried to get back together, but it failed after a few months. The children grew up, with posters of pop stars being replaced by Hollywood actors and footballers and then the walls starting to go bare as the elder two children, Joanne, still in a wheelchair, and Marie, left for college, much to the joy of the youngest, Tracy, who gained more and more wardrobe space.

At the start of 1999, Tracy, who was eight, complained of not feeling too well and being feverish. Mary put her to bed with some aspirin. A few hours later Tracy was complaining of muscle pains and a thumping headache.

Mary's first thoughts were that it was just some form of bug, but the paranoid voice at the back of the head of every parent was nagging her that it might be something far worse – meningitis.

'The thought that it could be this popped into my mind and once it was there, wouldn't leave. As the hours went on, part of me was convinced it was the worst but I was also terrified to take her to the doctors or the hospital for it to turn out that it was next to nothing and that the accusations of bad parenting and MSBP would spring up again, causing more grief for everyone.

'During the night she wasn't getting any better and had started vomiting, so I phoned Michael because I knew his partner had trained as a nurse.

'They rushed over and his partner said we should get her to the hospital as fast as we could because she was burning up and was in pain when you moved her head and neck.'

For Michael, it was an agonising time.

'Looking back, I was angry because I was concerned but I was screaming at Mary, calling her a bad parent and a lot of other things that I never should have, but I was really concerned. The minute I heard the word meningitis I just panicked.'

The dawn rush to the hospital confirmed the worst – Tracy had meningitis.

She was treated as well as could be expected, but over the coming days and weeks it became apparent that the infection had set in well.

Tracy was left with weakened hearing, occasional blurring episodes and found walking any distance an effort as she felt her limbs were unresponsive.

Mary feared the worst from social services: 'I thought I would lose her as they would point to my hesitation in getting her to hospital as bad parenting.

'There was an inquiry into it all and I was spoken to, but at the end of the day, no blame was attached to me by anyone. Except me. I tormented myself and still do. I look at pictures of how she used to be and how she is now.

'She's still my daughter and I love her, make no mistake about that, but her eyes seem a little duller now, as if some of the spark that made her who she was has gone out of her.

'There is no one else I can blame. People try to tell me that it all stems from the original accusations made by the doctor and that may be the case, but perhaps that doctor had a point as we ended up having to go with his therapy and treatment in the end.

'From that point on, the distrust of medical staff was all mine and because of that Tracy suffered and is afflicted for the rest of her life because of me.

'You could say that I wasn't a bad parent when I started out, but the accusations of being one actually turned me into one because my lack of trust of medical people led to my hesitation in dealing with them when Tracy was ill.

'The rest of the family don't blame me. Michael apologised for his comments made on the night, but what he said hit a raw nerve and he may have had a point. We rarely speak now.

'As I say, the family keep telling me that it's not my fault, but I know it is. In my own way I've condemned two of my daughters to pain and misery in their lives.'

Two

The History of MSBP

Most of the psychiatric conditions that we know of have been extensively researched over many decades. In these terms, MSBP is a relative new kid on the block, having only been named in 1977.

It is worthwhile considering where MSBP originates. As its name suggests, it stems from Munchausen Syndrome. But before we look at the syndrome, let us look at where the Munchausen part comes from.

Hieronymous Karl Fredrich von Munchausen was an 18th-century German baron and mercenary officer in the Russian cavalry. On his return from the Russo-Turkish wars, the baron entertained friends and neighbours with stories of his many exploits. Over time, his stories grew more and more expansive and finally quite outlandish. Munchausen became somewhat famous after a collection of his tales was published.

In 1794, at the age of 74, Munchausen married Bernhardine Brun, then 17 years old. It is said that on their wedding night, the baron retired early, and his bride spent the night dancing with another.

In 1795, Bernhardine gave birth to a son. Following the birth, it was whispered that 'the life of the Munchausen child will likely be short'. The boy, named Polle, died at approximately 1 year of age, in suspicious circumstances.

In 1877, an unusual behaviour pattern among young men appeared for a brief time in Europe. Adults were, through harming themselves, attempting to gain hospitalisation and treatment. At the time it was called mania operativa passiva.

Fast forward to 1951 to a respected English doctor in post-war Britain, Dr Richard Asher, writing in the esteemed medical journal *The Lancet*. His short article discussed three patients who were coming to hospital and claiming attention when nothing appeared to be wrong with them. The original report, written in a style that seems light-hearted, appears to have been written to alert medical staff in the newly formed National Health Service, where medical treatment was free of charge, to potential time and money wasters.

Dr Asher, who was in charge of the mental observation ward in Middlesex Hospital when he wrote the piece, coined the phrase that would come to define the condition when he compared the three to Baron von Munchausen.

While Dr Asher mentions that the patients are regular visitors, he never considers it possible that they are victims of multiple misdiagnoses and do actually have something wrong with them.

After this initial piece the topic was discussed in a number of medical journals, with other doctors claiming to know of patients who had nothing wrong with them but were looking for treatment for various ailments. In the letters pages of these journals, medical experts were quickly calling for registers to identify the Munchausen sufferers, letting hospitals know who they were so that they could be dismissed, as those claiming to be ill would give up looking for attention if they knew they were 'marked' people. The thought of what would have happened to these so-called attention seekers if they were actually ill is glossed over. Other suggestions included locking up anyone who appeared to be suffering from Munchausen Syndrome.

Within four years the syndrome had crossed the Atlantic and reached America, where, again through medical journals, doctors were warned of hospital 'bums' wasting time and resources.

Over the years, the accusations grew, with it being noted that most Munchausen 'sufferers' were from the less affluent part of society: drug addicts, many of whom were telling lies to get a fix, neurotics, malingerers and those with nowhere else to go.

It was also suggested at one point that perhaps Britain's National Health Service had encouraged the outbreak of the condition as it provided free treatment for those who need it, compared to systems in other countries where people have medical insurance.

During the 1960s very little was written on the topic but in the 1970s some people accused of having Munchausen Syndrome were diagnosed by psychiatrists as suffering from schizophrenia. (In the interests of clarity it is worth noting that schizophrenia does not mean that a person has, or is accused of having, multiple personalities. It is a condition that can include hearing imaginary voices, having delusions, social withdrawal and a significant and consistent change in overall personal behaviour.)

As the decade went on, more cases were discussed, but it was not until 1977 that an article in *The Lancet* described a variant of the condition. The report was written by Doctor, later Sir, Roy Meadow and it is here that the phrase that would haunt so many throughout the years originated:

'Some patients consistently produce false stories and fabricate evidence, so causing themselves needless hospital investigations and operations.

'Here are described patients who, by falsification, caused their children innumerable harmful hospital procedures – a sort of Munchausen syndrome by proxy.'

This first report dealt with two children – Kay and Charles. Over a period of several years Kay's parents provided fictitious information about her symptoms and tampered with her urine results and medical documents, leading to a number of surgical and radiological tests being carried out at a number of medical facilities.

Charles' tragic case was that he was given – orally and rectally – large doses of salt that led to his death, despite inquiries at three medical centres.

In his introduction to that article, Meadow notes: 'The behaviour of the parents of these two cases was similar in many ways, although the long-running saga of hospital care was reminiscent of the

Munchausen's syndrome, in these cases by proxy.'

Meadow does make at least one very good point in the article. Doctors do often take at face value what a parent tells them, as the bond of trust goes both ways. While no one can criticise the doctors for this, there seems to be an underlying message in the article that perhaps doctors should be more vigilant than they had been in the past.

It was also stated from the outset that he was convinced – and still is – that MSBP is a form of child abuse and not something that an adult who inflicts injuries on a child suffers from. He also later made the interesting point of tying it into conditions in the mother's life. If all was going well for her, then she could cope with life. If things were going badly, then MSBP could happen as a result.

Eventually there was more interest in MSBP than there had been in the original condition, but it did take a few years. Until the 1980s Meadow was the sole champion of the theory and he has confessed in his writings that some of the loneliest times in his professional life were in the early days of his work with MSBP because many other doctors and experts were not looking at it.

In part this was due to timing. The abuse of children was becoming more and more widespread and other matters like Sudden Infant Death Syndrome (SIDS) and Shaken Baby Syndrome were also coming to the attention of the public and medical professionals.

However, in America Drs Herbert Schreir and Judith Libow took an interest in MSBP and started publishing research into it.

In 1980, steps were taken to recognise MSBP as a condition when it was entered in that year's edition of the *Diagnostic and Statistical Manual of Mental Disorders (DSM-III)*, which is the industry bible for psychiatrists in America. It was classed under the generic name of 'factitious disorder'. In addition to the production of factitious physical symptoms, factitious psychological symptoms were recognised. This was actually the first time MSBP had been put forward as a psychiatric condition. Sir Roy had stressed in his original report that the work he had carried out classified MSBP as a physical condition and not a mental one. However, America saw it as a mental condition, hence its inclusion in the *DSM*.

Meadow himself disagreed with some of the findings of Schreir and Libow and wrote to them about this after they invited him to write something for them. What saw print was quite different from what the good doctor had written, as Schreir and Libow used the parts that praised their work and omitted all the criticisms.

Under the listing in the *DSM*, factitious psychological symptoms include factitious post-traumatic stress disorder, factitious psychosis, factitious depression, factitious rape and factitious bereavement.

MSBP was also given alternative names, normally Polle's syndrome and Meadow's syndrome, but neither stuck.

Meadow originally thought of the mother of the child as perpetrator and the child as simple victim, stating in 1982 that only children up to age six were used because a child older than that would be likely to reveal the deception. But in 1984 he amended this and said that he now believed that an older child could act as a willing accomplice of the mother, perhaps even setting off a pattern that could be repeated after the child reached adulthood and had children of its own.

Some of this reinforced what he had said in 1982 when he argued that after infancy the child may actually participate with the mother in the production of symptoms. He postulated that a very young child may do this by being aware of what the mother is doing but not volunteering that information to anyone.

He also pointed out then that as the child gets older there is more co-operation and complicity between mother and child. He put forward findings that seemed to suggest that as the child gets older the deception may be initiated by either one, with the other helping.

By 1985, Sir Roy had identified a group of areas that he felt should be looked at in any case of possible MSBP. These included studying the history of the patient to decide which events were likely to be fabricated and which ones were likely to be real. He also suggested looking at what he called 'the temporal relationship' between illnesses and the presence of the mother.

Doctors were also urged to check the details of the personal, social and family history that the mother had given and not to take her word for anything. They were advised to make contact with other family members and look for the motive behind the behaviour.

Meadow also pointed out that doctors should not rely on any form of psychological tests, as very often MSBP mothers appeared normal on them. He added that the psychologist and psychiatrist often write that they do not believe the mother could be practising the kinds of deception that have been discovered. This important point showed that personal interpretation of test results may have been biased by professional disbelief, something everyone had to be vigilant against.

In 1986, Schreir and Libow divided MSBP into three types, or stages.

They claimed that the first and least severe manifestation was a cry for help by the person committing the harm, moving on to more pain being caused to the child involved and finally a stage where the MSBP sufferer was almost addicted to going to see their doctor.

American experts and students of MSBP also added to Meadow's guidelines, and in 1986 published a far more comprehensive list of 16 points that they felt would help to distinguish between MSBP and any other form of illness, as well as seeing if someone was a genuine MSBP sufferer. The list, as published by Californian psychologist Deirdre Conway Rand, is as follows:

- Persistent or recurrent illnesses for which a cause cannot be found; child continues to be presented in victim role through newly 'remembered' allegations or 'add on' details.
- Discrepancies between history and clinical findings; history given of abuse that should produce physical findings, eg

repeated anal intercourse, yet medical exam negative; history includes episodes of abuse that are factually contradicted, eg in underground tunnels that can't be found by police.

- Symptoms and signs that do not occur when a child is away from the mother; child answers negatively about abuse away from mother/accuser.
- Unusual symptoms, signs or hospital cases that do not make clinical sense; abuse allegations that are bizarre or improbable; child appeared well-adjusted during the period when abuse was supposed to have occurred.
- A differential diagnosis consisting of disorders less common than Munchausen Syndrome by Proxy, eg allegations of multiple family members involved in incest, including grandparents.
- Persistent failure of a child to tolerate or respond to medical therapy without clear cause; child does not recover from abuse through therapy.
- A parent less concerned than the physician, sometimes comforting the medical staff; child recites allegations in a rote manner or eager to tell story.
- Repeated hospitalisations and vigorous medical evaluations of mother or child without definitive diagnoses; mother/accuser has child repeatedly evaluated for abuse and is dissatisfied with negative or equivocal results.
- A parent who is constantly at the child's bedside, excessively praises the staff, becomes overly attached to the staff, or becomes highly involved in the care of other patients; symbiotic, enmeshed relationship between mother and child, eg mother insists on staying in room for child's therapy interview.
- A parent who welcomes medical tests of her child, even when painful; mother/accuser seems to welcome repeated sexual assault exams and interrogations of child.
- Frequent comparisons of the child's medical problems to those of the parents; mother/accuser gives a history of having been molested as a child.

- The accusing adult seems to know more about what allegedly happened than does the child.
- Either mother/accuser or child distorts the truth, manipulates information by omission or fabrications of any kind, eg school, employment, medical, history.
- The accuser is more interested in building a case than in helping child deal with abuse and move on.
- There is a united front between mother and child, especially when the child is inappropriately alienated from the other parent, who is the accused.
- The accuser gives a history of herself having been molested as a child that is inconsistent with view of the family held by the majority of its members and with the family history as constructed by interviews with different family members.

It was also in the mid-eighties that American doctors noticed sex played a large part in many MSBP cases. It was found that mothers were claiming that their young child had been molested, taking the child for repeated pelvic exams that the mother observed, very often seeking a second opinion as they were not convinced by the first result.

Over the years this pattern continued, with divorced mothers and fathers admitting to examining the children themselves for sexual abuse after visits with the other parent, as well as taking them for post-visit medical exams.

Accusations of MSBP then started to find their way into the divorce court, with parents, normally fathers, claiming that the mother was harming their children. It was an effective tool in the war of trying to get custody of a child.

According to Mike Lewis, a lawyer involved in a number of cases at the time, it was a very powerful statement to make.

'Very few people knew what it was so you had a few moments to sum it up and that was it. The phrase that did the devastation was "where the parent suffers from a mental condition where they harm their children to get attention for themselves". You would follow this up with details of some of the things people accused of suffering from MSBP had done to their children.

'It didn't matter if an expert later came in and did their best to dismiss it because at the end of the day, it was the opening that stuck in people's minds – the possibility that this person, normally a woman, had harmed her own child. That brought out a strong, emotive response in people. Even those who didn't feel hatred for the MSBP-accused did feel that they should not have children left with them as they were obviously mentally ill.

'Also, psychiatrists had to admit that there was not a 100 per cent foolproof test that could be used to show someone had MSBP. It would be easy for people to believe someone did not have it when they actually did.

'As I say, if your client told you to put this forward so that he could get custody of the child or children, it went a long way to helping you.

'If it was used against you, then you were facing an uphill struggle.'

By the end of the decade, social work departments and the FBI were being given briefings on the matter. The FBI drew up a list of what it called MSBP warning signs. The FBI was also warning of a spin-off of MSBP called MSLE – Munchausen Syndrome in Law Enforcement, stating that 'the unique demands of the law enforcement profession create an atmosphere in which this type of disorder may be more common than in the general population'.

The FBI list of warning signs included:

- Unexplained, prolonged illness that is so extraordinary that it prompts medical professionals to remark that they've 'never seen anything like it before'.
- Repeat hospitalisations and medical evaluations without definitive diagnosis.
- Inappropriate or incongruous symptoms and/or signs that don't make medical sense.

- Persistent failure of a child to tolerate or respond to medical therapy without clear cause.
- Signs and symptoms that disappear when away from the parent. A differential diagnosis consisting of disorders less common than MSBP.
- Mothers who are not as concerned by their child's illness as the medical staff, who are constantly with their ill child in the hospital, who are at ease on the children's ward, and who form unusually close relationships with the medical staff.
- Families in which sudden, unexplained infant deaths have occurred and that have several members alleged to have serious medical disorders.
- Mothers with previous medical experience and who often give a medical history similar to the child's.
- Parent who welcomes medical tests of the child, even if painful.
- Increased parental uneasiness as child 'recovers' or approaches discharge.
- Parental attempts to convince the staff that the child is more ill than is apparent.

With organisations like the FBI giving credence to Meadow's hypothesis it garnered more and more respectability, and by the end of the 1980s MSBP was being looked at seriously as a condition in Britain and America, as well as other English-speaking countries.

No cases or conditions were reported from outside English-speaking countries though and MSBP was, on the whole, still a minority condition, not well known outside certain medical circles and those who came across it. The average person in the street was certainly unaware of it. That would change in the 1990s, with a number of court cases on both sides of the Atlantic forcing it into the public domain.

Three

Barbara, USA

Every mother only wants the best for her child. She wants them to be happy above all else: she may be frustrated at the paths they choose and regret the roads not taken, the partners not married, the babies never had, but at the end of the day if a mother feels she has done the best she can for her child, then she hopes that the child will grow up to be happy and well. Every mother wants this, but sometimes this simple desire can be enough to ensure the opposite.

Barbara from Texas only wanted the best for her children. In many ways her name and residence do not matter. She could be Susan from Iowa, Elisabeth from London, Mary from Auckland.

She could be you.

She has a normal home. Tidily decorated, but never quite tidy enough. Full of warmth, and not just from heat. The home of a person who cares. Her kitchen is like any other. Dishes to be done, food to be put away, notes on the fridge. The fridge looks like any other, but the contents of this fridge are unique.

Among the milk, the cheese, the normal food is a plastic bag. In the bag are three things: two bottles of glucola almost 20 years old and a note that warns: 'Don't even think about throwing these out.'

Those bottles are permanent reminders to Barbara of when trying to be the perfect mother led to the accusation of being the worst.

'I had three children, all sons, and as loved as any sons could be. I tried to treat them as equals, but the twins did get some extra attention from me because they had weak immune systems, which resulted in them catching everything and anything that was going around – colds, flu, anything – and keeping it longer than other children, meaning they missed lots of school days from second to fifth grade, but they were both active children, involved in the Scouts and doing everything children of that age should when they were able to.

'Then in the summer of 1983, just as the twins were getting over another poor winter and spring for health, one twin was informed he would not be allowed to return to school and start sixth grade unless he had a repeat MMR injection because his first one had been given one day prior to his first birthday, which was the recommended age for the injection at that time, but it has since risen to 15 months.

'At the time I thought that because his twin and their elder brother had had their shots a day or two after their first birthday, it seemed logical they also needed it.'

A mother's care, thinking about the future safeguarding of her sons, wanting them all to be as fit as possible – what mother wouldn't?

So, in August 1983 and just days before the family was due to leave for a holiday attending two amusement parks with lots of people and boiling, summer temperatures of 104–105 degrees, they stopped at the paediatric clinic office for a repeat MMR on all three boys.

It was the day when everything changed and while Barbara knows she did what she did from a desire to look after her boys, her light, proud Texan voice hesitates as she recalls the beginning of the nightmare.

'The decision to give all three boys the injection came from my desire to make sure they were all fully protected. As I say, I only wanted the best for my sons. Little did I know then that that decision was the beginning of the end of life as I thought I knew it or ever, in my very worst nightmare, might have predicted.

'Informing their father was not a problem, despite the fact that we had split up eight years earlier and he didn't always take an interest. Custody had never been a question for him or a big issue. The father had cleverly had his attorney draw up our separation agreement, which, because he had made sure it was not attached to the divorce decree, actually made the issue very murky if someone wanted to challenge custody. At the time of the split it had been clear the children would live with me, but there had been no court order ensuring it, but there had been no problems.'

However, problems of a different nature appeared not too long after that fateful day of the MMR treatments. Barbara's voice still betrays the pain she felt over her sons, 'my guys', becoming ill.

'When the change came, it came without warning and I saw my children go from happy, popular youngsters, Boy Scouts, who loved most sports, including the little-known game of soccer [football], running, biking and basketball into lethargic, pale alter-egos, shadows of their former selves.

'Morning after morning I'd try to wake my guys with a smile, encouraging them to go to school, trying to hide my worry at their sluggishness. Some mornings even getting them to wake up was a small miracle, actually getting them to school becoming a major miracle.

'The worry didn't stop when I got them to school for then I'd fret about what they had missed, if they could keep up, what other children would be saying.

'Their condition worsened and it got to the point where any skin colour that approached normal was welcome as they were becoming daily chameleons with the side effects of the MMR turning them blue, white, grey and many other deathly colours.'

Hindsight for a mother is a wonderful thing. Looking back almost 20 years with the benefit of two decades' more medical knowledge and expertise, Barbara can see that the children were suffering from forms of encephalopathy and conditions similar to mumps and meningitis, although Barbara to this day still feels that the measles and rubella components of the MMR injection were the main problem. She started to term life with her sons as the 'Invasion of the Body Snatchers'. The humour in the comment allowed her to hide some concern, but as any mother knows, hiding your concern from others is one thing; the one person you cannot hide it from is yourself. If anything, you fear the worst.

The children were stumbling through life; they were like victims of the sleepy sickness that swept Europe in the early decades of the 20th century. They were alive, but it was no life to lead.

And it was taking its toll.

'One twin had failed the fifth grade and was going to have to repeat because of too many absences, but as time went on I would have been happy to see him be in any grade at school, as the mornings worsened, with each boy eventually having to drop out of public and parochial school because there was no way to know if or when he would not be virtually comatose. I suggested a number of things, including work from home, but their studies were affected.

'We tried for as long as we could to carry on a semblance of normalcy. Many mornings, to the astonishment of the other mother in our car pool, I would pick up her two sons and dreamwalk through a semblance of what a normal life would have been if we had been allowed to have one.

'As much as this was so I did not let the others down, it was also a coping mechanism, for I knew if the normal world was still there my children could return to it and have happy, successful lives.

'However, fate was to deny me this simple right any mother should have and the children got progressively worse all fall and experts kept looking for illness but finding nothing.'

In 1983, media reporting was less sensationalist, patients' rights less of an issue, medical matters still more confined to medical journals than front-page exposés. Therefore Munchausen Syndrome by Proxy was not well known, but just as the children's ailment had slowly entered their lives only to end up dominating them, so would MSBP, as Barbara recalls.

'It was around October 1983, during one of the visits that I first heard a doctor hinting at some form of 'fictitious' illness, but I was more concerned with the children than that accusation to give it much thought.

'By Hallowe'en of that year, the sickest child and myself had an appointment to check his overall condition and especially to see if he had allergies, which some thought might be the cause of his discomfort.

'At that time, my medical knowledge was layman at best and I knew nothing of how a doctor should approach a patient, apart from the way doctors had treated me, but something struck me as strange over this doctor's so-called bedside manner when she did not appear to be overly interested in the child's overall condition and even less in his abdominal pain. Her biggest interest seemed to be "psychosocial history".

'I'll never forget her saying at two different times, "You don't want him to live with his father and I don't either", which I thought was strange coming from someone who knew nothing of my personal background – I certainly hadn't told her anything.

'Call it naiveté, but in those days I was like a rabbit caught in headlights when it came to asking others to explain what they meant. Perhaps I was respecting her position as a trusted and valued member of society or there was something else, but I did not ask her to elaborate on this comment, which I thought was very strange, and things got worse.'

Barbara was thinking that the aforementioned doctor not appearing to have much concern about her child's ailments was as bad as things could get, but things were about to get much worse, not only for her, but also for her child.

'I stayed at the hospital for the several days my son was to be there, but instead of feeling he was safe, my worry grew.

'At one point during the stay he was to be X-rayed and, as was procedure, he was to have only clear liquids several hours before. However, the schedule got delayed and he went 30 hours with nothing but liquids, most of which were very sugary and not good for him.

'He told me his stomach hurt really badly. He got his X-ray but next up was not food, but rather an appointment made for a psychiatrist the doctor sent for after she called him a liar for truthfully telling her that the scratch on his forehead happened when he was pushed in a haunted house, which I darn sure did not enter because while I may be from Texas, that is not my sort of thing.

'The psychiatrist asked if he would go to school if he was up for it. Having enjoyed school when he could go and being energetic, he said he would love to – if he was up for it, but that was rarely the case.

'Anyway, when the allergist announced, "He's not allergic at all", there were no apologies or surprise comments from the other allergist, who certainly had billed plenty for the tests and shots.

'More worryingly – and again, I only learned later that this could happen – there also was no mention of the huge likelihood that his system had been so stressed that it totally shut down.'

He may not have been allergic to anything, but in Barbara's eyes the family as a unit was getting allergic to doctors suggesting they see psychologists.

'As time went on and the guys' condition never improved, they started to get sick – sick of doctors parroting the "you look fine" line because they felt horrible and did not appreciate there seeming to be no effort to really find what was wrong.

'It got to the point where we figured that no one was looking for the right thing and that no matter what bizarre lab values came back from different places – and there were some very bizarre ones – we would always be told "they must have made a mistake in the lab".'

Barbara felt, like other mothers who have found themselves in similar circumstances, that if the evidence did not fit the theory it appeared to be discarded, instead of finding the theory that fitted the evidence present.

Then it got worse as the guys' father became more and more involved in the matter, with Barbara learning that he had indicated that 'I was vindictive'.

And while, decades on, some may feel they could look back and laugh at the more idiotic moments, that will never happen for Barbara as those days were spent wondering how bad things could get and knowing that every good day would be followed by many bad ones.

'It also got to the point that when the children said the same thing as me, they were accused of parroting me because I had turned them that way, though the irony, which to this day I cannot find the humour of, is that we were only telling the truth.

'However, no one was believing us and my belief that the truth would always set you free, something from my days as a reporter, was wearing very thin by this point.

'Three times one of the main paediatricians involved in the case thought he had a clue and would be able to help, but in the end he always doubted himself.

'We slogged through the fall with the guys eventually being in home school after they each dropped out of school.

'Then came Christmas and, for the first time, I was feeling so generous that I told the boys' father they could stay over Christmas Day with him and his wife.

'When they returned from Christmas vacation, a paediatrician suggested sending the eldest for a glucose tolerance test, which he flatlined [no heart activity showed on the monitor] – something I assumed was impossible. It turned out his system was sprung, just as his brother's must have been when he reacted to nothing he was documented to be allergic to.'

That clue was dismissed.

'Again, the sickest child was sent to a diagnostician in the state capital who, the child was amazed to notice, did not look at him at all when he palpated his abdomen.

'By this point, the guys were troopers at suffering, but they weren't that good that a decent doctor wouldn't have noticed the look of severe pain in his eyes and in the facial contortions. And still, there was said to be nothing wrong and that the guys should see a psychologist, though I couldn't work out what a psychologist was going to know about children turning blue, white and grey.

'The guys had pretty well had it with the idea of talking with any more people who thought they were faking. When they heard there was a blind psychiatrist in the area, they said they might consider going to him if they had to go anywhere because at least he would not be able to say, "Well, you look fine to me".

'By now I had little faith in the so-called experts who seemed reluctant to just admit when they didn't know something. However, one educational psychologist who tested the sickest child over the summer was a boon.

'She became our friend when, as part of one of the twin's educational testing, I was asked to fill in a lengthy assessment of the child, the family and other matters.

'Since it was a computer-graded exam, it wanted no caveats or essays or explanations: just the facts, ma'am.

'I knew I was in trouble when one of the early questions was about the child's birth order. Technically he is 13 minutes older than his identical twin. Try to explain that with just a yes or no.

'Another question was "Does the child have a hearing problem?" Well, yes, his hearing was so acute that everything was a distraction. I knew that my answers would not help her help him, so I wrote a letter to her which surprised and delighted her and it was she who, consulting with an out of town psychologist she trusted, told me to avoid going to many medical experts as regardless of what I did I would be tagged with some form of label.'

Barbara had as much idea about what that label would be as she did about what the imminent year of 1984 would be like. For her and her family, Big Brother had arrived early in the form of medical experts, but she was not sure that she could apply Big Brother's claims of love to the so-called experts. In fact, the only thing she was sure of was that she still wanted her children to try and have as much of a normal life as possible.

'I made sure that the boys were allowed to do as much as their energy permitted, knowing it made no sense to anyone else for children who could no longer predictably attend school regularly to join Scouts for a weekend if they could scrounge up what it took to do that.

'They tried to keep up with earning their Boy Scout badges and had less trouble getting to Scouts, which met at night, than to school. In the evenings I took them to the library and occasionally swimming. Anything healthy and helpful, but I knew the matter was not over yet. I could not shake the feeling that someone else's clock was ticking and I had this terrible feeling it was going to strike me.'

What struck Barbara in those early months of 1984 was the accusation of being a sufferer of MSBP. It's not a period in her life that she needs diaries or notes to recall. She remembers it as if it was yesterday – in fact she probably remembers it better than yesterday.

'It started in February 1984 when the accusation of harming my children to get attention was brought to the fore by the allegation and a report to the local child protection unit of Social Services and it hit home the following month when I went along with a suggestion to see an endocrinologist at a teaching hospital in North Carolina the day after the twins' 12th birthday.

'So on March 9 all three met with a person we believed was supposed to be an endocrinologist. It was only after I was thrown around by a very big county deputy and three hospital security people – not having raised my voice or hand – and the third child in that hospital for the serial alleged evaluation of each that I realised there really had been a set-up all along.

'While the guys were there, unknown to me, we were in a room in front of the nurses' station and we were under surveillance all the time. The other three mothers in the room, a couple of whom were there the entire time we were, kept asking, "What are the doctors doing to your children? They get so much worse while they are here."

'It was here that I pondered the fact that time and again perfectly clear physical evidence was dismissed and I wondered why until I researched other cases of mothers accused of being nasty to their children and I saw that very often any evidence which did not fit that theory would be dismissed.

'I realised that there were now serious accusations being thrown about accusing me of Munchausen Syndrome by Proxy, of harming my children as a way of getting attention. The idea was laughable, especially as I am comfortable with solitude, but it was not laughable once I realised others were believing this allegation.

'At the time there were no help groups for mothers falsely accused of harming their children and while there was a bevy of doctors and so-called professional child protectors – strangers nonetheless – singing the same song, friends and family – not all, but very nearly all – did not want to get involved, leaving me alone, and my cries that perhaps the doctors were wrong were met with me being told that doctors shouldn't be disrespected. Many were bowing to the inherent authority a doctor's rank carries; others had their own reasons for doubting me.

'Anyway, it turned out that the one we thought was an endocrinologist really headed the School of Social Medicine, having very recently completed his Ph.D. in public health to add to his paediatrics degree, but there was no help for the children, the main concern. My guys.

'To his chagrin, the eldest was told he would stay in the hospital first to be tested. For my alleged convenience, the other two would stay with their father.

'I tried playing dumb about what was happening to the children and I tried making lists and bringing copies of health problems I had found in print which seemed similar. I may have been occasionally exasperated, but I never was rude or dismissive and certainly not cruel – not as we were being treated.'

The eldest who went into that hospital and the eldest who came out of that hospital were practically two different people.

'He had once been a winning runner, but when he came out I doubt he could have run for a bus.

'In those six days he was in there he became a broken wreck of a youngster compared with the hopeful young man who began by believing that surely doctors in hospitals try to make you well, not find ways to create more sickness.'

He was given a glucose tolerance test, which was nothing if not imaginative.

'On one night he was given dinner with a regular cola drink. On the next night dinner came with a diet cola.

'There was a considerable difference between the several readings of the first night vs the second one. Gee, I thought, could that mean there was currently a problem with glucose tolerance? They ignored those variations in the numbers along with the fasting blood sugars of 142 and 145, which they said had no relation to possible diabetes.

'On the afternoon of his sixth day in the hospital, the big brother was in a foetal position on the bed in the middle of a three-hour nap.

'Four doctors marched in to pronounce him in fine fettle. I was horrified. I can't recall if he was even awake. I would have sold an arm for a camcorder, as it looked to all concerned as if the treatment had made him ill. The epidemiologist tried to convince the eldest about having a "conversion reaction", but this was too severe to be any reaction.

'While at home that weekend, I got a telephone call suggesting that I substitute the sicker twin for the one I had chosen next.

'I said I was not putting the twin who'd had the worst time in the position he always was in. My hope was that they would find the problem and he would not even have to go into the hospital.

'The first twin to go in is as affable as anyone in the world and amongst the family he was the most in denial about what was happening.

'He, in fact, was the only one who was "legally" required to have that repeat MMR. I still wonder how very different life would have been had I not tried to be such a good mother.

'When I visited him in the hospital, I had a hard time telling my son apart from the sheets, as the skin colour and sheet colour were practically the same. I asked the doctor to check his blood sugar.

The doctor said it would do no good because he'd been eating for 15 minutes, but I insisted.

'It turned out his blood sugar reading, never mind he'd been eating and drinking whatever gobs of sugar they'd given him to prove to me that he had no problem with overconsumption of sugar, was 52 [a very low score].

'It also turns out that the el cheapo glucola the hospital got on a low bid for its glucose tolerance tests was so vile the child vomited it back. So to get some glucose into his system, they gave my child a 2-litre bottle of straight cola, meaning the sugar was not the same composition as that in the glucola and it was certainly not the prescribed amount per weight for a proper test.

'The result was not what we expected. Instead of spiking at the first half hour, as test subjects are supposed to do, the reading was down and the doctor appeared to have no clue what that was about.

'In the meantime, I was spending time and money in the library trying to find answers for the questions they seemed hell-bent on not asking.

'During this, I knew my children were doing their best to be brave, but even they had to give in sometimes. A psychiatrist came to chat with the first twin in hospital and it must have been all of 20 seconds before he tossed his cookies, so to speak.

'Another moment I'll never forget is when the same twin had to write on his own chart "I have a headache", because no matter how often he told the nurse, she would not make a note of it.'

Then it got worse.

'By the time the last child is in place, things are minus no good. He lets me know that he does not think their father believes they are sick. I am still trying to convince him that the doctors will soon show him. We have all "agreed" to talk with psychologists and psychiatrists. The last child kept telling me he thought none of us was believed, and he was far more perceptive than I.

'As a last-ditch effort – now I know it was a true cut-throat gesture for a woman accused of Munchausen Syndrome by Proxy, but then it was all I could do – I told the resident who would perform the final glucose tolerance test that I would really like for one out of three to be done correctly, even though we both knew that this child was likely to vomit up the awful lemon-lime liquid as his twin had.

'The resident was truly impressed that I managed to come up with two bottles of precisely what I wanted, given to me at no charge by a local endocrinologist I never met, whose nurse told me where she would leave them after hours.

'No doubt it did not endear me to the resident when I opened a medical text I had purchased in their bookstore showing the proper amount of the glucola for a child's weight. All things considered, I probably should have let them do it wrong again. The boys and I were going to leave there separately, all of us with fabricated "psychological" labels, whatever had happened.'

Then the worst thing that can happen to any loving mother happened. Her guys were taken away from her. It was 30 March 1984. It was one of the saddest days of Barbara's life. It was also a day when she felt proud of her sons. A day of contradictions that only a mother could know or explain.

'March 30, 1984 is the day I want remembered as a tribute to the sons I reared to be the Eagle Scouts they became, while also being very regular rough and tumble guys and later in life active, productive and also sharing citizens despite all their problems. It was a day I was so proud of them.'

It was also the day, as they would say in novels, where the overall plot fell into place. Unfortunately this was no fiction, no bizarre story cooked up by Baron Munchausen. This was real life. Her life. Their lives.

'I was to attend a medical conference, which played out more like a military ambush than a meeting of concerned minds for the children.

'There were medical experts, doctors, nurses, the father and his wife, as well as myself.

'The whole meeting was geared to the conclusion that the children would be better off with their father than me and I was told that the children might need to live with their father in Virginia for six months. I agreed, at the time not realising that I was basically more or less volunteering to let them live there long enough to establish residency.

'When I rose after what seemed to be a very long reciting of anything but fact about the alleged effort to find what was wrong with my children, their father barked, "Sit down, Barbara". Sheeplike, I obeyed, but I did not stay for much more than a couple of minutes. I rose again and this was more like the appointed hour because as he moved towards the door before me, he opened it to admit a huge deputy and the three hospital security people. I guess it was the deputy who shoved some paper into my hands, which said the children would be taken off me.

'I wasn't thinking the straightest I ever had. I just had this great urge to see my child and I started out the door for his room, thinking that whatever this craziness was, he and I clearly needed to talk. I was hoping we could go alone upstairs to the playroom and just chat.

'So I'm walking to the room with my son in it, being pursued by an armed deputy, backup hospital security people, the children's father, his new wife and the medical staff, including two psychiatrists.

'And as I turned round and looked at one of the psychiatrists there, I wondered why there were so many. There I am, being pursued by all these people – what must people have been thinking about the situation and the person they are all chasing, I was thinking – and I suddenly realised that there was more to this than just my children.

'The penny dropped: it takes two psychiatrists to have you declared mentally unfit.

'Regardless of how we had split up I now saw that getting custody was not enough here. There was a personal angle between us to this. Surely he would not be wanting to still control the life of his children and that of his ex-wife? Surely there was more to this than just him wanting to dominate?

'A lot of little things suddenly fell into place, things that would later be backed up by speaking to others. This whole meeting was part of a scheme to make me fall to pieces, perhaps enough to be committed.

'For example, I was informed later the reason for the strong show of force was that he'd said I would fight and struggle and make a scene.

'It was also later revealed to me that the father had been approaching certain doctors to see why the twins had been so ill for so long and he had also made those comments about me being vindictive.

'The realisation was not the liberating Damascan blinding light that many claim these moments to be. I was lucid but dazed, shocked and horrified that a man who had been my closest companion, my friend, my mate, the father of my children, could do this.

'I remember going to the telephone and first calling the two children, who were with their aunt.

'The eldest burst into tears and the twin tried to be upbeat and assured me they'd be home some time, if not soon then maybe when they were 16. I was too stunned to drive home, so I spent a restless night in the nurses' old dorm, which, for $6 per night, let friends and family stay close to the hospital.

'In the morning I marched back up to the paediatric floor and took those bottles of glucola from the refrigerator and, ever since, they have been in my refrigerator. They are in a plastic bag. Inside the bag is a note to anyone who considers tossing out two ridiculous bottles from so many years ago. I think it says: "Don't even think about throwing these out."

'The children were kept away from me for 76 long days and nights where I worried about my guys and what was going on with them. Then a consent order was produced.

'One of the reasons for this was because of the so-called facility where my eldest was locked up. A judge held the head of the facility in contempt for not letting the locked-up child have civil rights, such as mail or a visitor.

'Our attorney called to say that he had a consent order and the children could come home. Now, many people might think that was the end of it. But when he read it, I said "no" because there was the false claim the children were "poisoned" by me and would not show affection to their father – to which I thought, Gosh, I wonder why? – and that they surely would be useless if they returned to me, but it was never going to work as things were going.

'The attorney managed to get it toned down a bit, and asked whether I'd rather have all the children back alive or play around with this chance for a while. That was pretty simple.

'It took a bit of work to get all the boys but when we got home there was one of the best heart-warming surprises of my life waiting for me. Unknown to us, the boys' friends and many mothers had tied yellow ribbons on our bushes and were waiting on the porch to give us the warmest welcome home I've ever known.

'Then in October, after putting me off for months and months, the attorney assigned to me by the one I had gone to finally acquiesced and took me to the Social Security office to look at my file.

'She had kept patting me on the head, telling me what good people these were and how they really cared about my children. She seemed to have a strong faith in the system and appeared unsure as to why others would not share that strong conviction.

'She went ballistic after reading the file because she realised that she had no time to try to mount a proper and decent defence in the timescale. Her faith in the system seemed to take a beating there.

'It was one of those moments that clearly did not require anything like "I told you so". I remained very quiet while she ranted all the way back to the office. What officially closed the matter was something I have not seen in any other case.

'Without my ever having to appear in any courtroom in Virginia, the attorney went to a judge and returned with two orders on October 29, 1984.

'One order gave me Virginia court-ordered custody. So, that

one was very important, but the other order appears to be unique.

'The other order indicated that the matter was not a "founded" case. The reason that is somewhat remarkable is that the judge had to reach across "separation" boundaries to write it and even to use the language used by an administrative agency which is under the executive branch of government, not judicial.'

After years of tests and accusations, it was found that her children had been affected by the MMR vaccination, which brought out a glucose intolerance in them.

But Barbara's story did not end with her victory. We will meet her again later on in this book and discover that this was only the beginning.

Four

MSBP Becomes Mainstream

While MSBP began as a theory in the late seventies and doctors started to use it in the eighties, it was not until the nineties that there was an explosion of cases that started to attract the public's attention, which in turn made more health care professionals aware of it, possibly leading to more and more diagnoses.

In America, the first trial of the decade was in 1991 when Patricia Stallings was convicted of murdering her three-month-old son by feeding him from a baby bottle laced with antifreeze. After Stallings was imprisoned she gave birth to another child, and it was discovered that both children had a rare genetic disorder, the symptoms of which were similar to the ingestion of antifreeze. Stallings was released.

In the UK it was the trial of Beverley Allitt that brought MSBP into the public forum. Allitt was a nurse who worked on Ward Four, a children's ward, at Grantham and Kesteven Hospital in Lincolnshire. In the spring of 1991 mysterious injuries started occurring to the children. Post-mortems, and scans and X-rays of those who survived revealed nothing.

The first incident took place on 21 February, which resulted in the death two days later of Liam Taylor, an eight-week-old baby. Over the next 60 days there were a number of inexplicable events. Nine children were injured and two more died before Monday 22 April when 15-month-old Claire Peck perished.

The following is a chronology of what happened as far as the experts can determine.

On 23 February, Liam Taylor, eight weeks old, died from a heart attack after being injected with insulin. He had been brought in with a chest infection, but it was not thought to be life threatening. Then, on 5 March, disabled Timothy Hardwick, 11, died from a heart attack after Allitt treated him for an epileptic fit. He relied on others to live because of his disabilities. He could hear but not communicate and he had difficulty processing visual information.

Five days later, on 10 March, Kayley Desmond, 14 months, stopped breathing after air was pumped into her armpit. She recovered, but only after being transferred to another hospital. Near the end of that month, on 28 March, non-diabetic Paul Crampton, five months, nearly died after being injected with an adult's dose of insulin. He only survived because he was transferred out of the hospital.

Two days later Bradley Gibson, five, was injected with insulin and had a non-fatal heart attack. The next day, 31 March, Henry Chan, two, stopped breathing but survived. The next fatality was on 5 April when Becky Phillips died after being injected with insulin. Becky's twin sister, Katie, almost suffocated on 7 April. The Phillips' mother, Susan, befriended Allitt, thanked her for saving Katie's life and asked her to be a godmother. In 1999 Katie's parents won £2.1 million compensation from the hospital to care for Katie, who now suffers from epilepsy and will be in a wheelchair for the rest of her life.

Back in 1991, on 9 April the heart of Michael Davidson, seven, stopped, but he survived.

13 April saw Chris Peasgood, eight months, almost suffocate, while on 16 April Chris King, nine months, stopped breathing but he too survived.

On 18 April Patrick Elstone, seven weeks, stopped breathing. He recovered but has brain damage.

Then on 22 April, Claire Peck, 15 months, died after being injected with lignocaine, an anaesthetic drug also used for cardiac arrest victims. She had been admitted for asthma.

Staff, some of whom could not even contemplate the possibility that a person was responsible for these events, nonetheless noted patterns in what was happening, but there was too little time and resources to mount a proper investigation, as the department was suffering badly from budget cuts, with only two nurses working the dayshift and one nurse on the nightshift.

On Friday 19 April, hospital consultant Dr Nelson Porter put what he thought were all the pieces of the puzzle together when he heard a lecture on MSBP. He got in touch with the hospital's powers that be, who were of the opinion that the work could begin on the following Monday. Undeterred, the doctor started work more or less immediately, looking at blood tests, samples from medical drips and any other evidence he could find. Among his findings were high levels of potassium in the tests, which was unusual.

He contacted a Detective Superintendent Stuart Clifton, who went through the medical reports and looked at staff rotas, noting that one name appeared more than any other: Beverley Allitt, who had been on shift every time there was an incident.

In November 1991 she was charged with the murders, with her trial taking place in February 1993 at Nottingham Crown Court. Allitt, who pleaded not guilty, did not attend all of the trial due to poor physical and mental health. She had been held in Rampton Psychiatric Hospital where she had lost 5 stone in weight through a form of anorexia and was also scalding herself and trying to eat broken glass.

The trial went on for almost three months and at the end of it the jury found Allitt guilty, with the judge, Justice Latham, sentencing the nurse to 13 life sentences, four for charges of murder and nine for grievous bodily harm.

There were two other accusations put to Allitt. Pensioner Dorothy Lowe suffered a hypoglycaemic attack on 27 April. She survived and Allitt was found not guilty of attempted murder.

The same thing happened on 4 August to Jonathan Jobson, 15. He survived and again, Allitt was found not guilty of attempted murder.

Allitt had been put on trial and found guilty but, as some

commentators on the case noted at the time, it was hard to hate a woman who was obviously psychologically ill. Just as the parents were suffering, so was she, but in a different way. That is not to excuse what she did, but the one thing never put on trial was the government of the day for allowing a National Health Service, the supposed envy of the world, to fall into a state where someone like Allitt was hired and then for there to be a lack of checks and security so that four children would die and nine others be severely injured. No one ever saw trial for that.

Considering that Porter's concerns were sparked by an MSBP lecture, the surprising thing is that the phrase was not Allitt's excuse for what happened. It was used by her defence lawyer instead, in an attempt to explain what she did. As far as anyone knows Allitt never used the phrase herself, and it was actually rejected by the court.

Even after the trial, Allitt remained newsworthy. In 1993 it was reported that she was opening steel paperclips and forcing them into her body. She hit the headlines again in 2001 when it was announced that she had plans to marry someone she had met inside.

Allitt and Scotsman Mark Heggie began a relationship in 1998. He had been held in Rampton after attacking 63-year-old Alison da Costa, breaking into her North London home after a drinking binge, battering her close to death and then drinking her blood. He admitted a charge of attempted murder while suffering from severe schizophrenia.

It will be a strange marriage for the couple as only once a fortnight are they allowed 20 minutes together under supervision. They are never left alone.

Parents of the children she harmed said they were disgusted by the news of her getting married but pointed out that they could do nothing about it as Allitt's right to marry was guaranteed under the Human Rights Act, which makes the European Convention on Human Rights part of UK law. The charter guarantees everyone the right to family life, including the right to marry.

A 1994 inquiry into Allitt and the hospital looked at staff failures and inadequate procedures, leading to a number of recommendations including the tightening up of nurses' recruitment, ensuring all applicants' sickness records are checked, better management of wards and more systematic investigation of untoward incidents.

It also called for a review of the role of paediatric pathologists where a death cannot be explained, and told coroners to send postmortem reports to consultants. The inquiry also dismissed the possibility that Allitt had MSBP.

In 1993, a British woman had her child taken from her in Arizona, America. Jan Brooks left her home town of Hull when she was 18 and moved to America, where she married, had two children and got divorced, then had a baby, Ashley, with another man. Ashley was a sickly child. She had a cold within a month of being born, cried all the time, had ear infections and as she grew, would rarely eat solids.

From September 1992 Ashley was in hospital for three months, being fed through a tube. She also had a hernia operation. At the end of the year she returned home to live with her mother, but still the child would not eat solids and she lost a lot of the weight she had gained in hospital. By March 1993, the ear infections had returned.

Jan admits to taking Ashley to the doctors a lot, something she put down to her UK upbringing, where it is more common to take a child to the doctor than just to order something over a counter, which is the standard practice in the US. While she may have been visiting the doctor for the best of reasons, nevertheless it was helping to build a case against her.

By May 1993, some people were beginning to suspect Jan of MSBP. She already had a reputation among hospital staff for questioning their decisions and both sides were frustrated in trying to help the little girl. By mid-May there were notes in Ashley's reports from staff mentioning concerns that Jan might be hindering Ashley's recovery.

Also in mid-May, a new doctor was appointed to Ashley, a Dr Mary Rimsza. Within two weeks Rimsza had put forward suggestions for foster placement for Ashley while Jan received a psychiatric evaluation. Ashley was placed at the East Valley Child Crisis Center.

Jan's confidence at this point was very low, but she received a boost when the doctor carrying out her psychological testing backed her, pointing out that she did not appear to have MSBP though she might be suffering from depression.

This doctor suggested that the feeding problems resulted from emotional distress and a lack of support for the mother. He also put forward his belief that the mother and child bonded well and saw no problems with them being reunited as long as Ashley was medically stable and there was counselling available, along with some classes in parenting for Jan.

A second opinion to this report advised the return of the child and the pair were reunited on 27 September, four months after being split up. They were closely watched by Child Protection Services (CPS) for six months, before being left alone.

Things have improved since then for the pair, but the four-month separation still haunts them, with Ashley panicking any time her mum is away, as if she is afraid that she is not coming back.

Again in the US, Julie Patrick may be the woman who, through tragedy, has helped more women accused of MSBP than any other. Prior to being accused of MSBP, she was already a prominent mother in America, having appeared on the top-rating ABC show *20/20* in 1994 when millions watched as open womb foetal surgery was carried out to save the life of Julie's unborn baby, Angela Grace, who was born nearly four months premature.

Julie quickly fell pregnant again and in 1995 gave birth to a son. While the birth was more straightforward than Angela Grace's, baby Philip was born with a number of birth defects such as malrotation of the bowels and craniosynostosis, and he also had trouble sleeping peacefully. Medical experts were baffled trying to work out what had happened to the child, and his parents e-mailed and faxed hundreds of doctors, health care professionals and medical centres in the hope of finding out what was wrong with their son.

After treating him for what was termed 'multiple infections' Vanderbilt Children's Hospital responded with an allegation of Munchausen Syndrome by Proxy, which led to Philip being confiscated. Once away from his family and in the care of the state, his condition rapidly deteriorated and he died in October 1996, aged 11 months, without his family near him.

An autopsy was carried out, and then reviewed to see if there was any need for police proceedings. The subsequent report, by Dr Bruce Levy, stated there was no evidence of MSBP and cleared Julie of any wrongdoing.

What Levy was critical of was the original autopsy, saying the report of it by then-acting medical examiner Dr Miles Jones was inadequate and that the autopsy was badly handled.

Kathleen Bush was America's Beverley Allitt. The Florida woman was not a nurse, but she was high profile and prominent, even more so than Julie Patrick. Home health care clerk Kathy and her young daughter Jennifer had met then-First Lady Hillary Clinton in 1994 when they had been lobbying for health insurance improvements.

They also testified at congressional hearings on health care costs and appeared on numerous TV shows highlighting the plight of the then four-year-old Jennifer. The mother and daughter's tales of Jennifer's illnesses and large, increasing medical bills put them in the national spotlight and they became, for a while, symbols for the movement for health care cost reform.

In 1996, however, it was revealed that Jennifer had been hospitalised 200 times and had had about 40 operations. The symptoms she was treated for included seizures, infections, diarrhoea and vomiting. It was claimed she suffered from neurogenic gastrointestinal pseudo-obstruction, which is a condition where the stomach does not digest solid food. It was also claimed that Jennifer had a defective immune system.

Among the operations was the removal of Jennifer's gall bladder, appendix and part of her intestines. She had a catheter surgically implanted in her chest, a tube running into her stomach and another to her intestines for feeding. The state started an investigation into Kathy and it was claimed that she gave Jennifer large doses of medication that were inappropriate, tampered with her feeding and falsified reports on medical charts.

The authorities pressed charges of aggravated child abuse and also fraud – due to their campaigning work for donations and free medical care for the sick child – in April 1996 and Jennifer was removed from Kathy's care and placed in protective custody.

The trial started in the second half of 1999, with her lawyer trying to throw out the allegations of MSBP. Robert C. Buschel told the court that MSBP was unsubstantiated and that the point was not to ask if Kathy had MSBP, the point was to ask if there had been child abuse. Her lawyers said there had not been, claiming Jennifer had been diagnosed with a gastrointestinal disorder caused by a deficiency in her immune system.

Judge for the case Judge Victor Tobin ruled that the prosecution, led by Assistant State Attorney Bob Nichols, was not allowed to specifically argue that Bush had MSBP.

Her prosecutors then went through the case without referring to MSBP by name, but presenting evidence that they claimed showed that Kathy had harmed Jennifer. However, at one point they did mention MSBP, with Kathy's lawyers unsuccessfully calling for a mistrial because of it.

During the trial, some doctors said they had seen test results that showed something was wrong with Jennifer's intestines that could not have been caused by Kathy. Other medical experts took the opposite view however, saying they believed that the health problems were caused by the mother.

Jennifer's adult brother Jason told the court that Jennifer pulled the tubes from her body because she wanted to be a normal little girl and that it was not because of anything their mother did. Jason, a Marine, said that Kathy did everything she could to help Jennifer and did not do anything to hurt her.

At another point in the trial there was some light relief, which was embarrassing for the prosecution, when the State Attorney's Office put the medical records of dead baseball legend Joe DiMaggio in evidence by mistake.

A nurse who cared for Jennifer for six years said that she had visited the Bushes more than 300 times and had never seen any signs of abuse towards Jennifer. The nurse, Robin Helfan, also said that Jennifer had been showing some signs of improving, eating more solids like McDonald's Chicken McNuggets and pizzas.

Two people who did not give evidence were Kathy and Jennifer.

In closing, Bush's lawyer argued that the case against Kathy was circumstantial, based on nothing more than 'innuendo, gossip and supposition'.

However, countering that, the prosecution said that strange incidents seemed to follow Kathy and Jennifer around from hospital to hospital and state to state. The prosecution also pointed out that in the three years since Jennifer had been taken out of her mother's care, she had only had a few colds and broken a limb while playing sports, nothing else.

In October 1999, the jury told the judge they needed some time to reach a verdict. Judge Tobin felt this was because they were having trouble trying to work out a sentence.

In the end though, they did not need too long, coming to a verdict within the first week of the month. That verdict was guilty on both charges.

Juror Steve Jordan later revealed that MSBP had only been mentioned by name a few times during the jury's deliberations, as they concentrated on treating the case as straightforward child abuse.

Conviction came in January 2000, with Kathy being sentenced to five years in prison, and another five years on probation.

Her case is currently under appeal. The basis for the appeal rests on a number of points, including the fact that the jury was not allowed to see all of the 33,000 pages of Jennifer's medical records that were entered into evidence and that the defence was not allowed to present testimony from a family therapist who treated Jennifer or from a woman who said the same nurse who accused Bush of harming her daughter also accused her of MSBP.

Jennifer, now a pretty teenager, has yet to be allowed to return home to her father, Craig, who to this day maintains his wife's innocence. The cost of legal action has seen the Bushes declared bankrupt but Craig says they will continue to fight, not only for his wife's innocence but also for the return of their daughter.

As Kathy's case was ongoing Julie Patrick set up the Mothers Against Munchausen Syndrome by Proxy Allegations (MAMA) Web site, which, among its many articles, put up what is regarded by many as the best riposte to MSBP allegations.

The MAMA site quickly became one of the best-known sites on the topic and its team of experts looked at the accusations and offered credible alternatives to the possibility that MSBP exists. It goes through them logically and shoots down most of the possibilities that were suggested in guidelines like those drawn up by the FBI (see Chapter 2).

A child who has one or more medical problems that do not respond to treatment or that follow an unusual course that is persistent, puzzling and unexplained.

This characteristic, with its many 'or's', would apply to anyone who has a medical syndrome. There are literally thousands of current syndromes, with new ones being identified each year. Each child who fits into a syndrome has more than one medical problem! Until the syndrome is found to be matching others, it is bizarre, puzzling and persistent. Many of the syndromes do not have an identified gene and this can make diagnosis difficult.

Physical or laboratory findings that are highly unusual, discrepant with history, or physically or clinically impossible.

This is dependent on the interpretation of the doctor and his experience. The discrepancy in history may be due to the way in which the history was obtained and if the questions were asked in the same way as previous interviews. Also, a parent under stress might tend to exaggerate as a way of emphasising their alarm.

A parent, usually the mother, who appears to be medically knowledgeable and/or fascinated with medical details and hospital gossip, appears to enjoy the hospital environment and expresses interest in the details of other patients' problems.

Any concerned mother will take the initiative to learn as much as possible when faced with a child who is critically/chronically ill, especially if her child is yet undiagnosed. This is a hallmark of a concerned, advocating mother. On the other hand, if a mother has had a prolonged stay, it would be unusual for her not to connect with other parents as a means of mutual support and as a result share information about one another's children when that is the world they are living in. Also, there must be quite a few people interested in medical knowledge since the television is full of hit shows like *E.R.*, *Chicago Hope*, *Rescue 911*, *Medical Detectives* and so on.

A highly attentive parent who is reluctant to leave her child's side and who herself seems to require constant attention.

This is another characteristic that any good, loving and advocating mother would have. One would have to ask who is making the claim that the mother requires constant attention? Is it a disgruntled nurse or doctor? Any mother who is truly an advocate will always brush some of the medical staff the wrong way in her endeavour to make things better for her child.

A parent who appears to be unusually calm in the face of serious difficulties in her child's medical course while being highly supportive and encouraging of the physician, or one who is angry, devalues staff and demands further intervention, more procedures, second opinions and transfers to other, more sophisticated facilities.

Which is it? This characteristic describes a very broad array of emotion. Any mother who has spent much time in the hospital has learned that physicians are hesitant to discuss details if the mother seems emotionally unstable. Also, if a life-threatening event occurs, a mother may maintain a cool exterior, so as not to be escorted from the room. It is quickly learned that to be an effective advocate, you must keep calm. If the physician seems to care, the mother will feel gratitude and express it. There is nothing wrong with being ingratiating to a physician who shows compassion. If a child continues to remain undiagnosed, both the mother and staff can become exasperated. A mother will become desperate and angry if she suspects that the physician has given up and the child is needlessly remaining in the hospital without a clue when things might improve. Also, there was a day when seeking second or third opinions was recommended by the finest physicians!

The suspected parent may work in the health care field herself or profess interest in a health-related job.

Countless people work in the health care field! It is a known phenomenon that parents who have a child saved by medicine aspire to give back what was given to them. Also, the mother of a child who has endured a lengthy stay might wish to pursue a career in medicine as a way of feeling that her child's suffering resulted in something good. Certainly she would have the ability to empathise with others.

The signs and symptoms of a child's illness do not occur in the parent's absence (hospitalisation and careful monitoring may be necessary to establish this causal relationship).

It is obvious that a mother will notice things a nurse would not. A mother spends more than a single shift observing her child and so it is not uncommon that certain symptoms are better documented during a parent's presence. A doctor might see a patient for only 10 minutes per day. It depends on how 'in tune' the observer is. Some symptoms naturally improve towards the end of the first year, just about the time a child is taken into 'protective custody'.

A family history of similar sibling illness or unexplained sibling illness or death.

A syndrome many times will affect parents and siblings (either to a lesser or greater degree).

A parent with symptoms similar to her child's own medical problems or an illness history that itself is puzzling and unusual.

As stated above, a syndrome might be present in the family. The same syndrome might have more prominent symptoms in the child and the parents might examine their own medical history in hopes of helping to find a diagnosis and speed their child's own cure.

A suspected parent with an emotionally distant relationship with her spouse; the spouse often fails to visit the patient and has little contact with physicians, even when the child is hospitalised with serious illness.

A chronically/critically ill child is known to put stress on the best of marriages. It may appear to be a distant relationship, but the mother and father have very different roles during this time and each has a hard time identifying with the other's stresses. A father may be visiting on weekends while the physicians are off. During the week he has all the responsibility of a single parent, trying to keep a household functioning. Someone has to keep things together! Also, it is a fact that very few fathers spend much time in an ICU dept. A father might fear breaking down in front of others or feel that he is protecting himself from deeper heartbreak by not allowing himself to become too attached, worried that the child might die.

A parent who reports dramatic, negative events, such as house fires, burglaries, car accidents, that affect her and her family while her child is undergoing treatment.

When it rains, it pours. Tragedy seems to come in waves and this is usually due to the fact that stress keeps parents from concentrating on things they normally would be conscientious of. Also, this is again very broad, depending on the length of an illness from months to years; many things can happen in that time.

A parent who seems to have an insatiable need for adulation or who makes self-serving efforts at public acknowledgement of her abilities.

Again, who is the observer? Who is interpreting the mother's actions? Do they have an agenda? Is the observer someone disgruntled by a mom who is a good advocate and was the critic simply brushed the wrong way? Maybe the observer is envious. Most mothers who have benefited by support groups and/or charitable foundations will be asked to help in some way, whether it be by speaking at fundraisers or even allowing their kid to be a poster child. No one works harder in a cause than someone who has 'been through it'.

However, the accusations continued, but there were also proven examples of children suffering.

In 1997, Mary Bryk was the first adult to publish her experiences as a child at the hands of her mother – a nurse highly regarded in the community. Bryk's abuse began aged two, when her mother took her to hospital with an ankle injury that refused to heal. Over the next eight years, Bryk was hospitalised 28 times, had 24 operations, multiple transfusions and skin and bone grafts.

Her medical history ran to more than 400 pages. The true cause of her illnesses was that her mother used a hammer and infected her daughter's wounds, although her mother denied it.

Also in 1997, in California five-year-old Trevor Nolan died in hospital, just three weeks after CPS took him and his brother Wade, six, out of the custody of their mother, Dale Nolan-Dissell, and into the care of their father, Ed, and then foster parents. Trevor suffered from a rare illness called glycogen storage disease that required him to be fed through a tube from infancy.

Despite the fact that he was moved away from his mother no charges of abuse or MSBP were ever substantiated against Mrs Nolan-Dissell, who then started a law suit for negligence against CPS, the boys' father and the foster parents. The case was meant to go before a jury for trial in April 2000, but in October 1999 it was announced that without admitting liability, the CPS employees agreed to settle the case out of court for $700,000. They did this because they feared that a jury might have gone for a higher sum. It was also revealed that the foster parents agreed through the state to a settlement of $125,000.

It was never revealed how much Mr Nolan paid his by then ex-wife. All three payments came through insurance companies.

An American survey published in 1999 seemed to back the claims of those who say MSBP is a myth that results from poor or inaccurate diagnoses by doctors. The survey said that statistically people were more likely to die from prescription medication than an accident, as adverse drug reactions was the fourth-ranking cause of death in the United States after heart disease, cancer and strokes.

The figures supplied suggested that in America there were between 76,000 and 137,000 deaths a year, as well as 2.2 million serious nonterminal reactions. According to the survey, prescription deaths and injuries came in two categories: the drug having too strong an effect or the drug carrying out unexpected damage.

What was of real interest to the MSBP group was the revelation that if a drug damaged a liver, the death would be recorded as liver failure, not as a drug reaction causing the liver failure.

It was hoped a new millennium would see a change in the accusations of MSBP, but a case carried over from 1999 proved there would be no chance of that.

Little can be said about the case for legal reasons, but it involved a Scotswoman and other members of her family being accused of unlawfully detaining her nine-year-old daughter.

When the mother was diagnosed with MSBP by Professor David Southall and it looked as if the daughter was going to be taken into care, the grandmother took her out of Britain and then across Scotland for four weeks, evading the police.

The reason for them being on the run was that the mother's 14-year-old son was in care and the family was worried that he was being physically abused by the social workers in charge. Northumbria Police dismissed the allegations.

When the case went to trial and sentencing in July 2001, members of the family, including the parents, were jailed for periods of between six and nine months.

In 2000, in the journal *Pediatrics*, Dr Judith Libow wrote that doctors should also consider the possibility that children themselves are faking their illness and that the children should be better understood to prevent them suffering from any form of syndrome associated with faking illnesses. The doctor found that almost three-quarters of the children involved in MSBP cases were female.

Also in 2000 the Royal College of Paediatrics and Child Health set up a working party to evaluate the Munchausen's Syndrome by Proxy diagnosis. At the time of going to press, no verdict had been delivered.

Five

Marcia, Australia

Australia. A land of new beginnings. New dreams and new lives away from the old world. Australians are famous for their optimism and sunny outlook on life.

For Marcia though, being an Australian is something that she now wishes she could deny, for she feels her country has betrayed her more than she thought possible. It tried to take her children away from her and left her in a jail to be abused, assaulted and nearly destroyed. She may have got her children back, but she can never let go of these memories. Marcia's experience in jail is not unique and it is something that those in authority should remember when making their MSBP accusations.

'I never had any problems with my children early on in life. Indeed quite the opposite. I thought I had a dream life with my children, Ross and Andrea, and husband, Peter.

'It was when Ross turned eight – two years younger than his sister – that things started to change, as he seemed more prone to emotional outbursts. Not just the usual childish tantrums, but real screams. On more than one occasion in public I was asked if I could prove I was his mother as people were reporting Peter and I to store security, suspecting us of kidnapping him.

'We took him to a child psychiatrist and also a doctor, which ended with him being prescribed various drugs to try and calm him down, while they ran more tests and profiles on him.

'This never seemed to make much difference that I could see. However, Ross said that he did feel better but it was not long before he would complain of almost constant stomach pains, which I thought was him acting up to avoid going to school, where he was finding himself in a lot of trouble because of his outbursts.

'At first I had put it down to bullying, but as time went on the psychiatrist told us that Ross had said he liked staying at home because it was easier than school and he got more attention.

'In the parent counselling classes that we had been going to since the outbursts began we were being taught a behaviour management programme for him. Whenever Ross acted out at home he was to spend time out in the bathroom. The reason given was that for a child of eight the bathroom was a pretty boring place.

'We were also told since there was so much stress on the family already that what happened at school was to be dealt with by the school and left there. Under no circumstances was Ross to be punished for anything that happened at school when he was at home, though teachers still had to tell us what he did each day.

During this time Ross's behaviour had been progressively getting more and more out of control. He was expressing his anger in more destructive ways. He had broken a window by throwing a book through it. On one occasion he had attempted to attack his father. Peter told me about this when I returned home from a friend's house. Since the kids were already asleep for the night, I took what I had been told at face value and left it at that.

'The next morning when I got the children up to prepare them for school, Ross was more combative than usual. I could tell that he was very angry about something but did not initially relate it to what I had been told by Peter had happened the night before. When I confronted Ross on his behaviour he looked up at me and told me that I just did not know what was truly going on. At that point he turned around and pulled down his pants. After the initial confusion of what he was doing, I saw something I never believed to be possible. My son had been beaten to the point that he was so severely bruised you could not see any normal-looking skin from his upper thighs to his lower back. At first I could not breathe, then I grabbed him up in my arms, caught between rage and guilt that I had not been there to protect him. Ross told me that it would be all right. I could not believe that this child could actually believe that he deserved this in any way, shape or form. I turned to see Andrea standing there looking at us. She said that Daddy scared her the night before. I was so very confused, the only thing I knew for sure at that point was that I was angry at Peter for doing such a thing to these children.

'I decided to call Peter at work and confront him. When he picked up the phone I verbally attacked him for what he had done. I was shocked to realise that there was no remorse for his actions. Peter instead told me that I was not allowed to send Ross to school. He also told me that if I were to tell anyone both Ross and I would pay dearly for me doing this. I was very confused at this point. I felt as though my head were spinning and I could not stop what was happening. I suddenly realised that it was time for the kids to be in school.

'I asked Andrea if she felt up to going to school. She said it would help her to feel better if she were at school. Ross said that he was afraid to go to school. He explained that he was afraid if anyone had seen what had happened to him they would take his dad to jail. I gathered the kids together in the car in order to take Andrea to school.

'After dropping off Andrea at school, Ross and I went home. At home I searched my mind furiously trying to figure out what to do. I wanted so desperately to take my children and run in order to keep them protected from any more abuse at the hands of their father. I also wanted to know without a doubt that I would be able to feed, clothe and shelter them. This presented a problem in my mind – because of the verbal attacks from Peter against me I was pretty much convinced that there was no way I would be able to provide for my children what they needed in order to survive.

'During this time Ross approached me and told me that he was very afraid of his father. I looked at him with tears in my eyes and explained to him that I was trying to figure out what to do. I promised him that I would do whatever I could in order to protect him from this ever happening again. I had no idea how I was going to do this however.

'During the day, my friend Mary came down to talk to me. She immediately picked up on something being very wrong. Ross was playing in the living room when I was asked by her what was up. I looked up at her and told her I couldn't say. This confused her as we have been close for many years. She then continued to probe as to what was up. Ross got up and walked into the room with us and told Mary that I was not allowed to say anything about it. I asked him if he could tell Mary what it was I was not allowed to say. I knew since Mary was a foster mother she would have some answer as to what to do. I also knew that by law she was required to report what Ross was about to tell her. Ross told Mary that we did not know what to do about what had taken place but he was very scared of his father. Mary got a concerned look over her face and asked why he would be afraid of his father. Ross pulled his pants down somewhat and showed her his backside and explained what had taken place the night before while I was away.

'Mary looked very intently at his bruises and turned to me and told me that I had to get the kids out of that house. I explained that I had no idea what to do and where to go. I explained my fears of not being able to take care of the kids. I also told her that I did not know where to turn for help.

'Mary told me that she would try to help me figure out what to do and then left.

She later called and said that even though she did not agree with what Peter had done, she had seen Ross acting out and could see where Peter could lose control. She then instructed me as to how to act in the interim until we could figure out what to do. I honestly believed that she was going to try and help. I thought that what she was telling me to do would help to prevent any further occurrences of any beatings.

'We kept Ross off school until the bruising had healed

completely. Peter explained how sorry he was to Ross and also to me. He said it had never happened before, he had just snapped at his son's behaviour. He also said that if it happened again, he would leave himself without any need of encouragement.

'Ross continued to have behaviour problems both at home and at school. One afternoon, before Peter returned home from work, Ross had another episode of explosive behaviour.

'Andrea was at Mary's, playing with her daughter Susan, so we were alone in the house. When I tried to calm him down, he turned his rage on me. He was yelling and screaming at me at first. He then seemed to go over the edge as he physically attacked me. He would swing at me with his fists as he was attempting to kick me. I picked him up and took him into my bedroom, where I sat down on the bed with him in my arms. I turned him around and sat him on my lap. I wrapped my arms around his chest and pulled his back up against my body, trying to perform the Therapeutic Hold manoeuvre that Ross's therapist had taught me to do.

'He started kicking me in my shins as he continued to struggle to get away from me. I wrapped my legs around his to stop him from kicking me.

'At that point he started to thrust his head back, hitting me in the face repeatedly. During all of this he continued to struggle against my attempts to restrain him and calm him down. Within a matter of minutes he had me worn out, with no sign of him starting to tire at all. I knew I needed help and quickly. I tried to talk to him but this seemed to only incite him more. I told him if we could not get him to calm down I would have to get some help in doing so. He did not respond at all to anything. I already felt like I had been beaten severely by his rage, but I knew in order to get help I would have to let go of Ross and call for help on the phone. I knew if I were to do this, he would do something to hurt himself.

'I decided I would have to restrain him somehow, if only long enough to call for help. I tried to think quickly as to how to do this as safely as possible. I then came up with the idea to use the bed sheets as a makeshift straitjacket. I chose this as it would hold him comfortably and securely. I also thought it might have the calming effect that wrapping a newborn in this manner does. Since he was much larger than a newborn and also much stronger I also knew that would not be enough to hold him. I then chose to get the cloth belts from the family's bathrobes to secure him. Once I had managed to do this, I went to call for help. Ross was struggling to free himself and yelling profusely during this time. I first made an emergency call to Ross's therapist. Then I called Peter at work and told him what was going on. He told me he was going to come home immediately. After I got off the phone with Peter, the therapist called back and spoke to me briefly and decided that Ross needed to be seen by his psychiatrist immediately. She told me to work as well as I could to calm him down and she would put in a call to the psychiatrist for me and have her call me back.

'When I got off the phone, Ross had already freed himself and chose to sit down in my room beside the wall. I sat down on the floor beside him and started talking to him. He was breathing very heavily still but was also very concerned over what had happened. He saw the bruises that he had caused on me and apologised. I told him not to worry about it; at the time I was more concerned about him.

'He told me that he did not know why he had acted that way. I told him that I felt we needed to find out why.

'Not long before Peter returned home I received a call from the psychiatrist. I told her what had transpired and what Ross was doing at the moment. She spoke to me for a bit, having me explain everything in as much detail as possible. During this time Peter walked in. He sat on the edge of the bed while I finished talking to the psychiatrist. When I got off the phone I told him that she wanted Ross brought in to her office immediately. Peter decided that I had been through enough at that point and he would take him to her office.

'When Peter and Ross returned home from the psychiatrist's office, Peter informed me that they had decided that Ross would go into a mental hospital for evaluation.

'Peter had decided that we would take him in the morning versus that evening so that he could say goodbye to Andrea. Also, we needed to prepare for him to be in the hospital, both emotionally and physically. I wanted to pack some special things for him so that he would not feel so homesick and afraid. I hated that he had to go into the hospital but I also felt that I could do nothing more for him. I felt that I had failed him.

'The next morning we got up and got Andrea off to school. We then finished packing Ross up and then took him to the hospital. The admission process was very long and involved. They asked a lot of personal and involved questions. Most of the time Peter answered them. Whenever I would try to interject he would cut me off. Because of this he answered many questions incorrectly and I felt he made Ross's behaviour seem much worse than it actually was. Whenever Ross would try to answer questions for himself Peter would interrupt him and answer for him.

'When they got through the admission process they allowed us to walk over to the unit Ross would be staying in.

'The nurse showed us around along with Ross. We were then told what Ross could have and he was allowed to ask us to bring anything that was not considered potentially harmful. Ross made out a list of what he felt we had forgotten and gave it to me. We were then told when we could visit him. At that point we had to leave him there.

'Over the next few days Ross was visited whenever we were off work. Whenever I went to see him he was always glad to see me. The staff told me that he was doing well, other than he missed being home with his family. After the first days Ross was moved to the day programme for one week. Peter would take him in the morning and drop him off and we would take turns picking him up in the afternoons. Ross liked the treatment he received there. At the family session that we had before he returned home and back to school we were given more information about the doctors' findings. We were told that Ross had ADHD [attention deficit hyperactivity disorder] and intermittent explosive disorder.

'I sent Ross to school the next day. He was excited that morning to be returning to school as he missed his friends there and his teachers. When he returned home from school Ross was acting strange. When I asked him what was bothering him he would not discuss it with me.

'The next couple of days Ross woke up complaining of an upset stomach and did not go to school. After a couple of days of this I grew concerned about why this could be happening and made an appointment with his paediatrician. She determined that Ross was showing symptoms of either a nervous stomach or he was getting an upset stomach from the new medication he was on. She gave me a prescription for Tagamet and told me that he should be all right to return to school the next day.

'That afternoon when Andrea returned home from school I asked Ross if he felt up to going out and running some errands. I had put these off since he was not feeling well. He said that since he had taken the medication that the paediatrician had given him he felt much better. So we went out to do some errands. While out Ross said he was starting to feel bad again, so I took him back to the paediatrician, who said she could find nothing up with him.

'He sat down while I finished what I was doing when he told me [that he was starting to feel bad] and we then returned home. This would be the last time I would be returning home with all my children for quite some time.

'The next day I got up and got the children ready for school as I did every school morning. When I was getting ready to leave I turned and saw some of the Department of Family and Children services workers driving slowly down the road.

I asked Mary later that day if she knew what was going on, as they'd stopped in front of my house. She told me that she had no idea but she thought that I should talk with them, if for no other reason, she joked, than to stop me being paranoid.

'It turned out they spoke to me first, coming over as I left Mary's home. A red-head called Josephine said that they had some questions for me concerning my children's safety and asked if I could come down to the local police station to answer them. My first thought was that something had happened at school and I feared the worst. Mary saw all of this happening and said she would come down with me.

'At the station, I was led into the detectives' area and into a room. I was introduced to Joyce, a detective, and Richard, who also worked with the Family and Children services.

'They told me that they were investigating allegations of child abuse in the area and had some questions for me. I didn't see how I could help them unless someone was claiming my children were being abused. Then I started to think that this would explain the problems at school for Ross, so I co-operated fully with them, answering all their questions in detail.

'They then proceeded to question me about Ross's recent stay in the hospital.

'I immediately got suspicious of their intentions. I told them that he had been sent there for evaluation by his psychiatrist when Peter took him into her office. They requested more information about why he was admitted and once again I told them it had been the doctor's decision. They then went on to question me further about why Ross had not been in school more than one day since his release from the hospital. I told them that he had been feeling sick to his stomach and after a few days of this I had taken him to his paediatrician, who determined that the medication that he had been put on at the hospital was making his stomach upset and she had given him something to help him. I also told them that he was at school now. They told me that they knew he was. I then questioned them as to why they knew so much about my kids when they had told me they were investigating someone else.

'That was when they told me that they had an order to take my kids into custody and they were doing so because they believed that I had Munchausen's Syndrome by Proxy. I was aghast at this revelation. Since I knew about the so-called disorder, I knew that the children would have had to be taken to a medical doctor and medical hospital many times and given unnecessary treatments. I told them that they had overstepped their boundaries because the criteria for this had not happened and they were wrong.

'They insisted that this was the case and that they were taking the kids and I could fight them in court if I chose to.

'I was highly upset and crying at this point and asked to be able to see my children. They refused to allow this, telling me that since I was so upset it would only upset them to see me that way. At that point Joyce got up and left the room, leaving Richard in there alone with me.

'He asked me why I took the kids to the doctor so often. I couldn't believe what I had just heard. I looked at him and told him he needed to only see the kids' medical records to know that they actually went to the doctor less than most kids since they tended to be healthier than normal kids their age. I also added that Andrea saw the doctor very rarely her entire life for anything more than normal well-child visits. I sat in the room for a bit trying to compose myself before leaving.

'When I left I called Peter to tell him what had happened. Peter was shocked by what I told him and left work, telling me he would be home as soon as possible. I then called my mother and let her know what was going on. She left work to come meet me at my place.

'By the time I got home I was going into a type of shock from everything that had transpired. My mother arrived shortly after I returned home. I was very worried as to what could have been taking Peter so long to get home. My mother was obviously concerned about the kids but she seemed to be very focused on me. I did not realise how bad I actually looked at the time. I spent most of the rest of that day sitting on the couch staring off at nothing in particular. I was almost numb. Whenever I thought of my kids it felt as though someone had ripped my heart out of my chest. It was already apparent to me that I no longer cared about anything. I would have gladly let them do whatever it was that they wanted to do to me, I just wanted to know where my kids were and that they were safe. I wanted to know what they were telling them and if the children believed it.

'It was quite some time before Peter got home. When he did he told us that he had gone to the Department to see if he could find out what was going on. He told my mother and I that he had seen Andrea but not Ross. He said that Andrea had a glazed look in her eyes and was very scared. At first she would not go to him. He told her that mummy and daddy did not want them to take her away from us and that we would be doing everything possible to get her back. We were then told that the head of the Department came out and told him that they could have him arrested for being there. He pushed her to tell him why they were doing this as he knew that I had done nothing wrong to our children. She refused to talk to him about anything and reiterated that he needed to leave. He argued with her for a few minutes more and when he found that he was getting nowhere with it he left to come home. This information upset me so much more – to know that my baby was frightened and confused as to what was going on. I knew that all of us at the house were confused by the entire situation; I could not imagine what this could be doing to the kids. However, I was yet to find out what other things they were doing to traumatise the kids.

'Peter quickly called our lawyer, Paul. He made arrangements for us to meet with Paul the next morning to discuss what we needed to do to get the kids back.

'The rest of the evening was spent with me remaining on the couch. My mother and Peter were moving around quite a bit discussing options that they could come up with on their own and what they thought the next move would be for us. We knew that there was a court date set for the next Monday afternoon and we needed an attorney with us there. Peter and Mum started making something to eat while they were discussing things. They were very upset that they could not get me to eat or drink anything. My mother pushed me to eat and drink. She finally got me to drink some water but not much. I felt if I tried to put too much in my stomach I would get sick. I didn't really care at that point if I ever ate anything again, I just wanted my babies. I wanted to know that they were OK and safe. I could not understand what I could have done to make them take my kids from me. I knew that I had never hurt them. I also knew that Peter had, but it was me that they were claiming had hurt my kids, not him. I also knew that I could not tell anyone the truth since that would give them reason to keep the kids. I decided that whatever it took I would get my kids back and no one would stop me. Those people that took them were wrong and I would prove it. I was a good mother and no one was going to tell me otherwise.

'The next morning, I got up with Peter and got ready to go to Paul's office. I was still in that numb state that I had slipped into the day before. About the time that we were ready to leave a police car pulled up in the driveway. Out stepped two huge burly officers. I was still upstairs when Peter answered the door. I could hear them asking for me and Peter asking why. They told him they had a warrant for my arrest. I walked down the stairs knowing what was going to happen but also having no idea what I was about to face over the next few days. I felt like I was going to pass out at any moment. I tried to convince myself it was because I had not eaten anything, but I knew it was more than that. I knew that this would effectively keep our attention from trying to get help for our children. I told Peter as I passed him to focus totally on the kids and worry about me later.

'Peter was starting to get furious over the situation and when we got outside he was yelling at the officers. I am not sure what exactly he was saying. I remember thinking, here he goes, now he gets angry, when it will do no good. Now, of all times, he needed to contain himself, but instead he was yelling at two huge police officers. The officers were telling him to back off or they were going to arrest him also. Even though I was very weak from fear, I did manage to get Peter to back off and be quiet. I told him the kids didn't stand a chance if he were arrested too.

'When we arrived at the station, one of the officers, that I tagged Brutus, got out and pulled me out of the car, causing me to hit my head on the door frame. He then jerked me, almost dragging me into the station. I told him he was hurting me. His response was to tell me that no one would believe me, I was a Munchausen's mum, I lied about everything.

I was then led to a chair inside the station and was left there for a woman officer to start processing me. She seemed to have many things going on so the process seemed to take forever. I sat there for a while by myself as she did some paperwork. I did not speak and barely moved. As she observed this she seemed to be bothered by it. She asked me several times if I was OK. I would always reply "yes" but I am sure she could see that I thought what she was asking was quite out of the ordinary. How in the world could I possibly be OK? They had kidnapped my children and arrested me and up to this point I could not understand why. I knew what Munchausen's was supposed to be, but my children had not been badly ill for a few years.

'This was all very foreign to me and I had no idea as to what to expect. At one point a class of preschoolers was brought in to tour the jail and station. During this time I was placed in a holding cell. It was empty except for the trash that had been left in there. The place smelled of urine and some other things that I could not place. I tried to get up and walk around some but felt so weak that whenever I stood up I felt as though I would pass out.

'When they came to get me from the holding cell I was taken to be fingerprinted. During this whole time I did not say a word, stunned speechless by the entire process. I was then led back to the chair where I had originally been placed. The woman officer came back in and asked me some questions in order to fill out some paperwork. All of my answers were very brief and direct. She then went and got some kind of uniform and took me into another room, which had a shower and changing area. She had me strip off all of my clothes. She went through my clothes as she had me hand them to her. Once all of my clothes were off she had me turn away from her and then proceeded to do a cavity search. She then sprayed me with some kind of spray and told me to shower and make sure I got all of the spray off as it would irritate my skin and cause me to break out in hives if I did not. She then left after returning my panties and shoes. She took the rest of my clothes and put them in a bag. As I showered I cried about the humiliating experience I had just gone through. I tried my best to get all of the spray off. However, by that time I was shaking so badly I could hardly do anything effectively. After showering I dried myself and donned the uniform I was given. I then waited for the officer to return.

'When she returned I was taken to a cell block upstairs. I was given a blanket and was told they did not have any more pillows or mats since they had so many inmates at the time. I was then led into where the inmates were. At that time everyone was locked in their cells. I was put in a cell with two other women. One was rather small and very pretty and quiet. The other was very large, obviously not someone I would have ever met up with under any other circumstance. She was loud and very brash. I was told that since there were not enough beds I would have to sleep on the floor. When the guard locked the door, the larger woman immediately asked me what my name was and why I was there. I told her my name but said I had no idea what my charges were since no one had told me. She told me that her name was Lacy and what she was there for. I can't remember her exact charges but it had to do with endangering her children. As I listened to her talk, I knew immediately that I was afraid of her. She openly admitted to hurting her kids and this did not seem to bother her in the least. She also expressed that she preferred being in jail to being on the outside since they fed her and she didn't have to work. I could not comprehend this attitude at all. I already knew that I did not want to be in jail and would have preferred to not have ever seen the inside of one, ever. Dawn, on the other hand, was very nice and soft spoken. She said that she was waiting to be transferred to prison. She had been sentenced to three years. She seemed to be foreign to this environment, but had somehow managed to adjust. She however stayed very distant in her mannerisms. I could look into her eyes and see a very deep sadness that contained a lot of pain. She would eventually open up to me but she dealt with things that were very hard to talk about. I could also see that she would not talk in front of Lacy.

'After the brief exchanges the guards started serving lunches. I knew I needed to eat something even though I had no appetite. Lacy said that as far as jail food went, this place was very good. I looked over at Dawn when she said this and knew that wasn't saying much. They told me once the food was passed out they would let us out into the common area. I thought this would be good since the cell felt so confining. I had no idea though as to who or what I would meet when I left the cell. When they delivered the food and I had a chance to look at what was served I was aghast. There was something that looked like what you would find in a cowpat, an orange, stale bread and something completely unknown to me. I could not believe that anyone would think this was edible. Lacy told me the dark pile that you would easily mistake for excrement from a cow was in actuality peanut butter and one of the better things served. I figured it was high time I went on a diet at that point. There was no way I was going to eat what was before me. Dawn convinced me that I did need to eat at least part of what they served. She told me that if I did not eat then they had beaten me. I knew I could not give them that satisfaction as I knew already that was what they wanted more than anything. I ate the bread and the orange. The other inmates quickly ate whatever I chose not to eat.

'When we were allowed to go out into the common area, I was overwhelmed by the other inmates. They were very interested in finding out who I was and what the situation was. I did not talk too much but decided it would be best to at least try to be somewhat sociable. I am sure it was very apparent that I had no idea as to how to fit in with these people and also that I was terrified of the situation I was in. I never asked questions about the others' situations, as I really did not want to know. I did find everyone to be very forthcoming about their charges or what they were convicted of. Many there could not believe that I really did not have any idea of what my charges were. They were certain that I really did not have any idea though.

'It did not take me long to determine who it was there that I did not want to be around. Unfortunately those were the very people that seemed to be around me. There was one woman there who looked as though she would be pretty despite her masculine features. However, at the time she was severely bruised all over her face from a fight. She said it was due in part to the police and also someone that she had an altercation with. She made me very nervous by her demeanour. She was very aggressive and showed dominance over the other inmates.

'Another inmate that I would have preferred to avoid was a young girl aged 17. She had a wild look about her. She was not overly tall but she was overweight. She had been charged with a violent crime, which I never heard the details of, but I did know they were planning on trying her as an adult. When she approached me, she would get right up in my face to talk to me. She got right to the point, asking me about my sexuality. She told me that she preferred men but women had their good points also. I made it clear I had no sexual interest in women but explained that I did not have any opinions about how others should conduct themselves sexually.

'Sharon was another person who introduced herself very quickly. She was of average size, very upbeat and obviously had a gift of enjoying herself despite her situation. She had been charged as an accessory to armed robbery and some minor drug charges. There was a woman there who was four months pregnant who was waiting to be transferred to prison. She was nice but very quiet and kept to herself.

'Another woman there who I immediately had concerns about was the one that they called the house mother. She took care of making sure that the inmates had supplies that were needed for personal situations. She was quiet also but demanded respect from everyone around her. There were others there who I will talk about later, as they came to be involved with me.

'After everyone had eaten lunch we were allowed to stay in the common area. There was a TV there but I could not make out what was being said on it. I soon learned that whenever people talked at a normal level the sound would bounce off the walls and get progressively louder and more confusing. It did not take long for this to get to me. I found that if I went into the cell the noise was not as bad. Dawn had given me a couple of her magazines to read. I decided to sit in the cell and read in order to avoid the confusing noise in the common area. Not long after I went into the cell Lacy decided to come in. She told me there would be a couple of people joining us. I did not know whether or not it was allowed for other inmates to go into cells that were not their own, but I did not think too much about it. Lacy also told me that we needed to be careful not to shut the doors all the way as they would lock us in. Two other inmates soon came in. One was the 17-year-old, the other was the woman who had bruises on her face. As they came in they pushed the door to but did not completely close it. Before they had the door completely closed I saw one person standing outside the door but could not make out who it was.

'The younger girl sat down beside me and started asking me questions about my sexual experiences. I tried to avoid the questions by telling her that I had never done anything that would be worth writing the magazines about. She then pushed further, asking if I had ever been with a woman. I started to move away from her and told her I had never had any interest in that kind of thing. She then moved closer to me again. I started to get more concerned about the situation than I had initially been. I started to stand up in order to leave the cell, when Lacy stood up beside me and told me that there was no need to leave, they just wanted to talk. I told her I had no interest in where this conversation was leading and I wanted to go out into the common area. At that point Lacy and the other woman grabbed my arm and forced me to sit back down. Lacy then grabbed my hands as the younger one started to undo my uniform. I started to scream for the guards, when one of them stuck something in my mouth. Lacy continued to restrain my hands and moved around behind me.

'She whispered in my ear that it would be no use to fight them as they were much bigger than I was, which was true. She then told me that they could and would do anything to me that they wanted to and I would not tell anyone if I wanted to live. I continued to try to resist, hoping that someone would come by and notice something was going on and stop it. I was kicking my feet to try to push the other two away from me as they removed the top of my uniform. Lacy then pulled my arms up over my head, forcing me to lie down on the floor as the other two pulled the uniform further down and used it to restrain my legs. I then spat out the thing that they had stuffed in my mouth. Lacy quickly changed positions, using her knees to hold down my wrists.

She then grabbed the cloth that I had spat out and put it back in my mouth. She used the ends of this to hold my head down to the floor.

'The youngest one then started to run her hands along my sides as she straddled my body. She started talking about how much I was going to enjoy what she was doing. I continued to struggle against them but it was becoming more and more apparent that they were too strong. I relaxed for a moment and realised that Lacy had loosened her grip of the cloth that she had been holding in my mouth. I looked up to see where her attention was. She was watching the 17-year-old and was saying something to the other woman. I started to raise my head and twist to once again try to free myself. Lacy then grabbed my hair and slammed my head down on the concrete floor. For a moment I had trouble focusing. I could feel someone grabbing my breast. Another one was pulling my panties down. I could feel someone's knees digging into my shins and hands moving up the insides of my thighs. During this time Lacy was starting to laugh. She was telling me that after this

I would never be satisfied by a man. I tried once again to move my head. Lacy again took me by the hair, lifted up my head and slammed it on the floor. I was then told if I moved again I would be hurt even worse. It would be best for me to lie back and enjoy what they were doing. I could feel myself drifting but I do not think I ever passed out. It seemed that the room was spinning, but I could still feel what they were doing. I could feel teeth on my nipples biting me.

'I could feel the pain of someone pushing their hand up inside me. I could hear them laughing and telling each other what they were going to do next. Lacy switched positions with the 17-year-old and proceeded to bite my breast. Somehow I was able to mentally refuse to feel the pain any more. I felt as though I was standing in the room watching everything that was happening. I could see them hitting my body, then biting me and pushing their hands up inside me. I did not know how it was that I could see what was happening from the angle I was seeing it. I just knew that I was and I could no longer feel what they were doing. I felt as though I was watching a movie and I tried to convince myself that this was in fact what was happening. I tried very hard to imagine this scene to be something from a story and not something that was actually happening to me. I watched myself being held down on the floor, having things done to me that I never imagined possible. I watched them finish and pull my clothes back up on me. I could see the bite marks they had left on my legs and breasts. Once they finished they got up and left me there like a limp doll.

'I knew I wouldn't be able to take much more of this. Perhaps then it was fortunate that within days I was informed that I was to be released as the charges had been dropped and my family returned to me.

'The charges were dropped on the grounds that there was not enough proof that I was anything but an over-zealous mother who would take her children, especially Ross, to the doctors at the first sign of illness.

'I was informed by my lawyer that there were reprimands and

inquiries into the behaviour of those involved in my case but nothing that ever amounted to a formal apology to me or my family. He told me that was because at the end of the day, the official public line was that they had acted in the best interests of the children, something which I laughingly disagree with.

'If I sound bitter I believe that I have good reason to be. My family was nearly split up, I was almost driven insane and my son's professional diagnoses ignored just so some people could say they were trying to make things better, poking their noses in where they were not invited.

'To this day, Ross still has episodes, but with the medication he is on, they are less severe. He still has the occasional stomach cramp, but the doctors tell us that is because of the medicine and that the best they can do is try to minimise the discomfort because he needs to be on the other medicine to keep him calm. He will never grow out of the episodes, but we will always be a family there to look after him, regardless of the best efforts of others to split us up.'

Six

The Argument For MSBP

For any medical theory to take hold, it must have champions. If no one had been convinced by the 1977 article in *The Lancet* then it might all have been dismissed, but the theory did take root in the brains of some.

Obviously the first of these was Roy Meadow himself.

His medical career began when he graduated from Oxford University in 1960. He spent his early years in general practice before becoming a registrar in paediatrics. It was once he became a registrar that he started studying the effects on parents of having a child in hospital, and for his work he was awarded the prestigious Donald Paterson prize of the British Paediatric Association in 1968.

It was at the end of the 1960s that he started to develop an interest in paediatric nephrology, the specialist study of the liver in children. He then went to Birmingham to continue his work by studying the epidemiology of urinary tract infections in children with Professor Richard White. In 1970, he went to Leeds to be a senior lecturer in paediatrics. Here he seemed to find a niche, working well with colleagues and producing a series of lecture notes that are still regarded as among the best students can have.

A few years into his tenure at Leeds he set up a paediatric nephrology service, with interests as diverse as enuresis and renal failure. It was during this time that he discovered what he felt was a clinical syndrome where parents were fabricating their child's illness, leading to many unnecessary investigations and even, on occasion, the child's death.

He wrote up his findings and they were published in the 13 August 1977 edition of *The Lancet*, titled 'The Hinterlands of Child Abuse'. This was the article that started the MSBP bandwagon rolling.

In 1980 Meadow found himself invited to take up the prestigious position of chair of paediatrics at St James's University Hospital, Leeds. During the next 14 years he continued to teach and build his reputation, to the extent that fellow professors were coming to his lectures to see what he was teaching.

He also developed his clear and easy writing style, which made him a popular author of many textbooks. He also became editor of the major paediatric journal *Archives of Disease in Childhood*.

In 1994 he was elected to the Presidency of the British Paediatric Association. This was a time when medical paediatrics was developing rapidly and the drive for an independent College of Paediatrics was becoming unstoppable.

Armed with a mandate from members of the British Paediatric Association he pursued the target of a separate college and the Privy Council was pleased to grant a Royal Charter to The Royal College of Paediatrics and Child Health in 1996. Meadow became its first president.

Dr Roy Meadow became Sir Roy Meadow when he received a knighthood in the New Year's Honours List 1997 for his services to child health. In 1997 he also announced that he would be retiring from the chair of paediatrics at the end of the academic year 1997/98.

He has always been passionate about protecting children and while he rarely does media interviews he did provide glimpses into his thoughts in the *Archives of Disease in Childhood*.

In one article he said:

'Even though the number of infants categorised as sudden infant death syndrome has fallen below 400 a year, it is a national scandal that we accept a situation in which so many young children die from unexplained causes. If one out of every 1,000 21-year-olds died suddenly and unexpectedly, without an identifiable cause, there would be a national outcry.'

He has also called for the abandoning of the term 'cot death', or at least its alteration. He feels the phrase 'unexplained death' or 'undetermined death' should be used instead, as cot death is a convenient tag to put on deaths that are not explainable on first investigation. Ironically many have also said the same about MSBP.

Sir Roy has also been involved as an expert witness on a number of child abuse cases, but some of his testimony was shot down in a case involving an English woman, Sally Clark. Sally was appealing convictions of killing her 11-week-old son Christopher in December 1996 and her younger son, eight-week-old Harry, a year later.

Sally, from Wilmslow, Cheshire, has always insisted that her children died in a rare tragedy as a result of so-called cot death or Sudden Infant Death Syndrome but the prosecution alleged instead that Sally, suffering from depression during the period in which she killed her sons, either smothered or shook the children to death.

She had been found guilty and given a life sentence. She appealed in 2000. Central to this, Sally's lawyers argued, was the evidence of Sir Roy. Sir Roy said that the chances of two children from the same family dying of SIDS were 73 million to one.

But Sally's legal team claimed that the true figure was closer to one in 8,500, producing evidence from the Foundation for the Study of Infant Deaths that a double cot death happens in Britain once every 18 months.

In an 82-page written judgment, Lord Justice Henry, chairman of the appeal panel, said the trial judge should have dismissed the 73-million-to-one figure as a 'distraction' and not directed the jury to consider the prosecution statistics. But the Court of Appeal judge said the point was of 'minimal significance', adding that the combined weight of medical and circumstantial evidence against Mrs Clark made her conviction still a certainty.

While Sir Roy is credited as the man who invented the term Munchausen Syndrome by Proxy, it is worth remembering that he never called it a mental illness or psychiatric condition. All he stated was that in his opinion there was a form of child abuse taking place where an adult was abusing a child to gain attention.

After Sir Roy, the person most commonly associated with MSBP in the UK is Professor David Southall. Over the years, Professor Southall, like Sir Roy, has found himself called as an expert witness in cases involving accusations of MSBP.

Like Sir Roy, Professor Southall was regarded as one of the best and brightest in his field. He has been awarded government recognition for his groundbreaking eight-bed paediatric intensive care unit. He was a paediatrician working at the cutting edge of child health in London when he was headhunted by North Staffordshire Hospital, where he accepted a position in 1992.

As well as his excellent reputation, Professor Southall took two controversial techniques to North Staffordshire Hospital, techniques which, over the years, have seen him hailed as a saint and saviour of lives and simultaneously damned as a dangerous man who has put lives in danger and split families for no reason.

The two controversial techniques were CNEP (continuous negative extrathoracic pressure) tanks to help premature babies with a chest illness and covert video surveillance to trap parents in the act of assaulting their children.

CNEP is a specialised system where babies suffering from chest illness are placed in chambers where the pressure is then lowered to enable their chests to expand and so breathe unaided. The doctors who believe in the technique say it removes the need for traditional ventilation under which an air tube is pushed down the infant's throat, with a risk of trauma and infection. Southall's work in this area ran from 1989 until 1993.

The video surveillance involved hidden cameras in rooms where children were with their parents, in an attempt to find people suffering from MSBP. The videos showed a catalogue of abuse including suffocation, kicking, deliberate fractures and poisoning.

Among the more harrowing scenes, a young mother was filmed breaking her three-month-old daughter's arm. In others, parents have been caught trying to smother their children with pillows.

Southall had been videoing since 1987 and it was this, along with CNEP, that would cause much controversy in the closing years of the 20th century.

In 1992 he argued that recordings of physiological data from a baby suffering suffocation may, in time, be as good as video surveillance for establishing the guilt of abusers.

In 1993 he led research into allegations that a wide range of treatments were being carried out on children without any form of painkiller. He discovered that at the Royal Brompton Hospital, south-west London, about a third of the procedures witnessed were done without a pain reliever or sedative being given. In some cases minor surgical work involving restitching wounds or cutting out a piece of muscle tissue for analysis was undertaken without painkillers.

He said at the time:

'You see a state of frozen watchfulness on their faces when doctors or nurses approach, which we recognise from children we know have been assaulted by their parents. Babies and children under five are unable to express pain as adults or older children can. They can't say, "I want you to stop." '

Also in 1993 he started to call for the government to do more for the children in war-torn areas like Sarajevo. He made this plea after travelling there and discovering for himself how bad the conditions were. He was awarded an OBE for his work in this field.

The covert video work ended after it was publicly revealed after a court action. The court action happened when North Staffordshire Hospital obtained a High Court injunction banning disclosure of confidential research material relating to the covert video surveillance, material that had been copied without permission by a charity worker who wanted inquiries into the methods used by Professor Southall.

When news of the method was revealed, he said:

'We have had to discontinue covert surveillance not because I believe there is anything wrong with the technique but because of the adverse publicity.

'Parents now know that if their children come into my care they may be subject to surveillance and that makes the method impracticable.'

The professor claimed surveillance was justified by the fact that protection orders had been issued in all but one of the cases in which he had used the technique and 33 people had been prosecuted because of it.

He said:

'If these children had not been protected their lives would have been devastated. They were subject to all manner of physical and emotional abuse.'

He also felt that it was the only way to get the evidence necessary to protect the child, regardless of how people, including himself, felt about it.

'It is rather like bugging someone's telephone or infiltrating a spy into an organisation. No one likes the technique but it is the only way to get the evidence.'

Many doctors at the time said Southall's motives may have been correct but his procedure certainly was not. Some wondered if it was not some form of entrapment and also something that could damage the crucial patient/doctor relationship.

The Royal College of Paediatrics and Child Health backed the use of the technique though, to the surprise of many, saying that it was vindicated in exceptional circumstances where evidence was not otherwise available.

In 1998, it was revealed that there was to be an inquiry into the CNEP trials. Among the matters the inquiry was to look at was the length of the experiments and also some claims by parents that they had not given proper consent for the tests to take place. It was revealed that out of the 122 children who took part in the trials, 28 died and 15 suffered brain damage. Parents also claimed that they were not told of the risk of brain damage and the fact that the treatment was experimental until they read an article by

Professor Southall and a colleague for a US medical magazine.

The inquiry became known as the Griffiths Inquiry, after its chairman, Professor Rod Griffiths. The report pointed to three areas where there had been problems. It claimed that the local Research Ethical Committee, which was supposed to ensure the tests were run properly, was slightly complacent and failed to take advice on its decisions. Once it approved Professor Southall's proposals for an experiment it failed to ensure it was conducted as he promised.

Second, it was felt that Professor Southall failed to monitor the tests properly. It was often left to overworked and undertrained nursing staff to gain consent from parents for their babies to take part.

Lastly, the report stated that the hospital had no guidelines on running medical research, and although national guidelines were followed, these were inadequate.

Professor Griffiths did not make a ruling on claims that consent had not always been sought properly. All the report said on this matter was:

'What was clearly totally unacceptable to them [the parents] was the apparent lack of adequate explanation, of choice and of consequent properly elicited and recorded consent.'

The report also did not address claims that the treatment had led to brain damage and death in some cases, but added that insufficient work had been carried out to see if the treatment did cause damage. Griffiths himself later added that the mortality rates among a similar study group were broadly similar to those in the CNEP trials.

Professor Southall has admitted privately that some of the criticism over the last few years has left him shaken but he also insists that the need to protect children from their own parents at times can overrule any civil liberties issue.

In an interview with *The Sentinel* newspaper Professor Southall said:

'I don't like being criticised but I can understand where it is coming from. A lot of people cannot believe parents could do such awful things to their children and they don't want to believe it.

'One has to look at it in a fatalistic way – that anyone involved in child abuse work will be criticised.

'Have I been intimidated by events? No. Would I become involved in child protection if I had my time again? Unequivocally, yes.'

When asked about MSBP he said:

'We see hundreds of babies a year who have been referred to us because of unexplained cyanotic attacks [when a child goes blue].

'MSBP is always the last option when we have done all the physiological tests. But then we have to go out of our way to find objective evidence that will stand up in court.'

In October 2001 Southall was cleared of all charges and reinstated by the hospital trust.

Of the covert video surveillance, the medical director at North Staffordshire NHS Trust, Pat Chipping, said, 'There is no evidence of inappropriate use. It was always undertaken following full investigation and when all other diagnostic approaches had been used.

'Professor Southall has always acted in a way that promoted the best interests of children under his care.'

It was also stated that accusations that CNEP tanks caused death or brain damage could not be substantiated on the basis of the current information.

Southall was also cleared of any cavalier attitude towards obtaining the consent of parents.

Professor Southall did not respond to requests for an interview for this book, but a colleague who worked closely with him stated:

'I've seen the stuff on the Internet that calls him a monster and torturer. David Southall is neither.

'He has always pushed himself and those around him to find ways to help alleviate the suffering of children. Yes, there may have been controversy surrounding the work he did, but he did it for noble reasons and let's also remember that he has been praised by a lot of parents. He is not this universal monster that people like to portray him as. He could easily never have pioneered the work that he did and remained in a steady, comfortable job, but he did what he did because he was concerned for the health of children.'

In 2000 Professor Southall's Child Advocacy International charity received a £150,000 lottery grant to fight child abuse in developing countries.

As noted in Chapter 2, in America MSBP is seen as a psychiatric condition, not a physical one.

The main proponents of this theory are Herbert Schreir and Marc Feldman.

Dr Schreir, who is director of psychiatry at the Children's Hospital Medical Center in Oakland, California is one of America's leading experts on the syndrome and has investigated more than 30 cases in the past 10 years, many of which have come to court and have seen Schreir called as an expert witness.

He has various research and clinical interests, but particularly cognitive and developmental disorders in very young children, including autism, non-verbal learning disabilities, Tourette's syndrome and the conditions that go along with Tourette's, like obsessive-compulsive disorder (OCD), attention deficit disorder and severe behavioural problems resulting from abuse.

He has written a number of works on MSBP, the most famous being *Hurting for Love*, which in the early 1990s suggested that the syndrome was much more common than the experts believed at that time. He also argued in a 1992 report in the Bulletin of the Menninger Clinic that there is some evidence that MSBP-prone mothers have experienced childhood deprivation or abandonment.

Dr Schreir and the co-author of *Hurting for Love*, Dr Judith Libow, also reported on a questionnaire to 1,258 American paediatricians asking for details of cases that may show signs of

MSBP. They received 316 replies describing a total of 465 cases.

He said: 'We believe that many of them are not being diagnosed. For example, when cases are exposed there is often an older child who died a few years earlier in mysterious circumstances.

'Existing theories about why these women torture children with unnecessary drugs and enemas and catheters usually claim it is to do with seeking attention.

'But that doesn't begin to explain their sadistic glee at moments of crisis, and until we understand what is really happening we won't be in a position to detect it easily.'

These cases, which may involve mothers or women caring for children, are regarded as a mystery, he says, because all the attention focuses on how a woman could do such things to a child.

'But that is to miss the point. The key is that the woman regards the child as a fetishistic object, valuable only as a means of manipulating her relationship with the doctor, whom she considers to be a parent substitute. This is not a sexual relationship. What these women want is both recognition and revenge. To get it they make both the child and the doctor their victims.'

Caught in the middle of this is the doctor, who, according to Schreir, is normally unaware of what is going on. Schreir has noted that in each of his cases there has been an intense relationship between the woman and the doctor treating the child, but the doctor was unable to see what was happening.

'These women leave a lot of clues. They tell lies that can be easily checked; they do things it's easy to detect like cutting feeding tubes. But the doctors involved don't notice.'

Schreir originally believed that there may be some attempt at seeking a sexual connection with the doctor, but he later decided it was very often nothing to do with sex; it was more about security and being recognised as a person and having some worth.

According to Schreir, 'We have found many cases of neglect in the MSBP sufferers. As little girls they all had feelings of being humiliated and not valued. Then at some point they got the attention they craved from a doctor or someone medical and became driven by two opposing forces, sadistic and masochistic.'

They want security and recognition from the doctor – a parent substitute who can be male or female.

'These women are impostors. They are playing the role of the caring mother or nurse and they do it brilliantly.

'Doctors can also go completely unaware of all of this as they also flatter and admire them. Until you've encountered one, you can't believe how convincing they are.'

According to Schreir the other problem doctors face with MSBP is that the abuser will often change the way in which they inflict pain on their victim, perplexing the doctor as to how all the different injuries are appearing in one person without a connection.

'Doctors like to be challenged, but many also don't like to admit they can't sort something out, so their confidence is taking dents while they try to sort out the illness mystery, which can mean they are not suspecting the child or person is being abused. It is not the first thought in many people's minds.

'This and doctors working independently are major reasons MSBP goes undetected – because doctors feel a need to be smart and independent. If they have a problem they tend to try to solve it on their own. When we are called in the first thing we do is to get the doctors involved to discuss it together and suddenly what they couldn't see before becomes clear.'

Alabama-based Dr Feldman is also regarded as an expert in MSBP. His popular Internet site (address on page 206) is packed with details on the condition, but he also deals with the more straightforward Munchausen Syndrome (MS).

On his Web site he details in simple terms what he believes MSBP and MS are:

'They [sufferers] deliberately mislead others into thinking they (or their children) have serious medical or psychological problems, often resulting in extraordinary numbers of medication trials, diagnostic tests, hospitalisations and even surgery... that they know aren't really needed. In short, factitious disorders, like malingering, involve "disease forgery".

'They may induce an actual illness – eg by injecting themselves or their child with bacteria to cause a raging infection.

'In unusual variants, some seek the hero or victim role, rather than the sick role. The good news is that knowledge about factitious disorders has been increasing exponentially.'

One of Feldman's most lasting contributions to the debate has been his identification of a new variant of the syndrome – Munchausen By Internet.

In this form of the disorder, people use online message boards, chat rooms, e-mail lists and newsgroups to make false claims about illness. He believes that some people concoct elaborate ruses, complete with fake personal histories, phoney lab and X-ray reports, invented conversations with physicians and even fictitious citations from medical journals just to try to get attention.

The lack of face-to-face communication on the Internet helps with this, according to Feldman:

'People on the Internet are faceless and anonymous. You don't have the same accountability that you have in face-to-face interactions.

'I think the threshold for deception is lower on the Internet and people who mislead others may dismiss it as playfulness on their part and of no particular consequence, but my research shows that's not how it's perceived by the victims.'

Feldman believes there are a number of issues involved here.

'These issues are expanding in importance as patients increasingly use the Internet to seek tele-advice from people they have not actually met. With fictitious illness cases, people have wasted time and emotional energy at one end, but even worse, at the other extreme you could have people who may have made decisions about their own health care based on false information put out by those who are faking it.'

Feldman has spotted a number of ways of finding out if a person's illness is genuine or not.

'These include long or frequent posts from someone claiming to be in the throes of acute illness or near-fatal bouts with illness alternating with miraculous recoveries, continual dramatic events in the person's life, especially when someone else becomes the group's new focus of attention, complaints that other group members are not supportive enough and warnings that this is undermining the person's health.

'There can also be posts that are ostensibly made on behalf of the person by friends or family members, but which have the same grammatical errors, misspellings and individual writing style.'

Meadow, Southall, Schreir and Feldman are not the only doctors who believe in MSBP, but they are the experts referred to constantly in articles across the world. They are the vanguard of the pro-MSBP movement.

Seven

Terri, Canada

For some parents, the accusation of MSBP comes after they themselves have been ill for a lengthy period. Some doctors have speculated that this is because of a progression from the original Munchausen Syndrome, while others postulate that the mental illness comes after a physical illness or that the person is so used to getting the attention that they had when they were ill that they will do anything to get it back.

This is what happened to Terri in Canada. She first became ill through her work and from that, plus a lot of bad luck, her life was turned upside down and she had her children taken away from her. Here is her story.

'It was about a week before my wedding to my husband John in March 1996 when everything started. I was working as a nurse at one of the local hospitals and an agitated patient, who turned out to have mental difficulties, threw me over a bed. I injured my lower back and bruised some ribs due to a collision with a support on the side of the bed.

'I was told to rest it for a month but obviously I couldn't, as I wanted to put the finishing touches to the wedding. I was of the opinion that I'd only ever have one wedding so I wanted it to be perfect.

'On our wedding day I was still pretty sore and I spent most of the day trying to cover up how much pain I was in.

'I went back to work the week after we got married, but during March my back got progressively worse until I could no longer stand up without severe pain radiating down my legs. The doctors put me on complete bed rest for the next few months. They said they could find little wrong with me, but they said it may be some nerve damage as judging by the way I was acting, they felt there was no way I could be faking it, though one did suggest that there may be some psychosomatic connection to wedding stress. They also told me that the rest would be good for another reason – I was pregnant.

'Not long after we found out about the baby, I started having severe pains and some bleeding. I was in a great deal of pain and very scared. John took me to the hospital and the doctor said that he was concerned I might have a tubule pregnancy and wanted to do surgery to be sure that this was not the case. I was worried about the surgery because if I did not have a tubule pregnancy, the surgery could cause me to lose the baby.

'I ended up agreeing to the surgery and they found out that there was no tubule pregnancy. They determined that I had more than likely lost a twin to the child I was still pregnant with.

'They put me on bed rest until the bleeding stopped. Of course, I was still on bed rest from the back injury. As I was recuperating from the surgery I started experiencing really heavy morning sickness. It wasn't long before John started getting concerned that I was not having typical morning sickness. On one occasion I tried to get up for something and passed out in his arms. At that point he decided enough was enough and had me go to the doctor.

'That trip to the doctor wound up buying me a couple of days in the hospital. The doctors started me on some drugs to alleviate the nausea. The drugs worked perfectly for the nausea; however, it was not fully explained to me that there could be side effects for the baby.

'When I entered my second trimester of pregnancy I started to feel great. I still had not gained any weight because I had been so sick, but that was soon to change. I was beginning to enjoy being pregnant and the doctors were encouraging me to eat more than I would have normally eaten.

'As the second trimester went on, feeling great soon became a distant memory. I started having what seemed to be complications with the pregnancy. I started getting very sharp, hard pains in my abdomen. On a few occasions they were so bad that I was taken to the hospital. Most of the time they would go away on their own, but when they didn't I would be doubled over in pain. When I was taken to the hospital they would very often administer narcotics and tell me that I was experiencing what were known as Braxton-Hicks contractions. This of course confused me as I had always been told that these contractions were fairly mild and I knew that my tolerance for pain had always been very high. I believed that the doctors must know what they were talking about, since I had never experienced anything like this before. Between what I was told were Braxton-Hicks contractions and my back injury, which still lingered, I was again put on bed rest.

'In the beginning of November 1996, I developed pre-eclampsia. When I went into the doctor's office, my blood pressure was so high they immediately sent me to the hospital. I did not realise that they had planned on admitting me at the time. They initially did some tests on me and the baby. Then they filled me in on what was going on. I was upset at the news but they told me that they were planning on delivering the baby as soon as possible.

'In the hospital, they closely followed my blood pressure. They also started trying to induce me. I was under the impression that that meant I would have the baby rather quickly. That was not the case and I was there for over a week. They continued to try to induce me for several more days, until I finally went into labour on my own. I was quite comfortable and all for it remaining that way, but it wasn't to be. About noon or so the pains started getting very bad. They were still far enough apart that I could get a break in between. By 3 pm this was no longer the case; by 4 pm I was for any drug they would give me. They gave me nothing, no matter how much I begged.

'They told me they were afraid if they gave me anything it would stop the labour. Imagine that they thought I cared! I was given some drugs but mainly to stop me being sick or feeling nauseous, so I was in agony.

'The ordeal eventually ended and Nick made his entrance into the world weighing 5 lb 1 oz.

'There seemed to be no complications for either of us from the birth and we left hospital a few days later and went back to our apartment, which was now crowded.

'Nick was a very happy and active baby. He never lagged behind developmentally – he just did not grow. I had this beautiful baby boy that was such a joy to my life. The only real problem was that he spat up a lot of his food but we always made sure that he ate and swallowed at every meal.

'He hardly ever cried and was always happy. He was so easy-going also. I could take him anywhere and do anything with him without worry. I just wished that I could make this perfect little child I had grow, but I could not.

'Nick had stopped gaining weight. I took him into the paediatrician's office and the first thing I was asked was whether or not he was premature. I was stunned that the doctor felt this to be a possibility. I never considered that people might think this the case with him. I told the doctor that he was born only one week before his due date. The doctor was more concerned about this than anyone else had been. He immediately called a paediatric specialist and set up an appointment for the next week. I left the doctor's office more upset than I had been about Nick's condition ever.

'The next week I took Nick to the specialist, who ended up suggesting a barrage of tests for him. He was a real trooper about everything but I could not stand to see what they were putting him through.

'As the results came in the doctor kept me abreast of what was going on and what the tests said. The first conclusion they came to was that Nick suffered from some form of gastroesophageal reflux, which is a condition where a child splashes or pushes stomach contents backwards up into the oesophagus and sometimes out the mouth.

'I was told if you compared Nick's reflux to him being a

baseball player he would make the all-star team with no problem, it was so developed. On one visit to the doctor I told him that Nick was no longer spitting up. I thought that this was a good sign; however, I was told otherwise. It was explained to me that the reflux had not gone away and that just the fact that he was refluxing still would burn up a great many calories. About this time what was told to me was showing itself by the fact that Nick was starting to lose weight.

'The doctor started to try to prepare me for the possibility that Nick would need to have surgery. The thought of the doctors cutting my son was horrifying to me. I could not imagine having to put this precious baby through that kind of torture. I dreaded the possibility of surgery for him but John and I both knew that it was probably inevitable at this point.

'During the time that we were going through all this turmoil with Nick, I came down with severe sickness. They wound up putting me in the hospital again, this time for a week. There were some comments from friends and family that I was constantly faking it for attention, but these were just jokes, though it would be an accusation thrown back at me by the doctors and so-called experts in years to come.

'On Hallowe'en of 1997 however, things took a drastic turn for the worst. That afternoon I was sitting in the reclining chair with Nick playing on the floor beside me. When he tired he fell asleep right beside the chair. Since I felt so tired myself I did not get up to put him in his crib. After some time I looked down and saw that his face had turned blue. I reached down to check him and discovered that my baby had stopped breathing. I was terrified. I immediately got on the floor with him and tried to shake him and get him to start breathing. I was yelling his name and shaking him, until I realised that he was not responding. I checked his pulse and could easily tell that it was still there. I then started giving him breaths; it seemed to take forever. I continued until he started to make efforts to breathe on his own. When he started trying to breathe he also started to spit up. He struggled for a time and then started to cry. At that point I realised that I too was crying and shaking. I was so afraid that I was going to lose my child. I grabbed him up and called the paediatrician's office to let them know what was going on. They told me to get him to the hospital immediately. I grabbed a few things and called both my mother and John to let them know what was up and took off with Nick to the hospital. I got stuck in the afternoon rush hour every direction I tried. It took me over an hour to get somewhere that should have taken 15 minutes or less. I could not believe I could not get my child to the hospital. I was very afraid that he would stop breathing again and I would be stuck on the side of the road with him with no way of getting help. About halfway to the hospital I finally considered that calling the EMTs [Emergency Medical Teams] would have been a better plan of action than the one that I had chosen.

'When I finally arrived at the hospital my mother was waiting for us. Nick looked better than he had when we had left but he still looked rather pale and my mother took note of this. While we were still in the emergency room, John arrived. He tried to play with Nick as my mother tried in vain to calm me. Nick would smile at him but was apparently not his usual cheerful self.

'The doctors chose to admit Nick and continued to run yet more tests on him. When we were settled somewhat in Nick's room, they came up to take what was called a blood gas on him. I could not take all the poking and prodding they were doing to him any longer, so I walked outside to take a break from all the stress. After I returned upstairs to the room, my mother left to go home, leaving John, Nick and I alone for a bit. John was relatively calm, which was good as I was at my wits' end.

'Before John left to go home the doctors came by to check on Nick and told us that at that point they felt that surgery would be inevitable. They explained that they felt that Nick's episode was due to him refluxing and it blocking his airway. I was questioned as to how long Nick was not breathing, which I could not answer because I had not been witness to when he actually stopped.

'They then explained that what Nick had experienced was called apnoea. They ordered an apnoea monitor for him, which he was to remain on at all times. This device would measure his heart rate and breathing. It also had the capability to record any episodes of his heart rate going too high or too low and any apnoeas.

'I felt better knowing that there was something to alert us if he was to stop breathing again. John wanted me to go home with him and try to get some sleep. However, I could not bear to leave my child all alone in that scary hospital. I stayed with him almost the entire time he was in the hospital, only leaving for very short periods of time.

'Nick was in the hospital about a week before they did the surgery on him. During that time they performed several more tests on him and arranged a surgical consult. I was still suffering from some sickness during this time, so the nurses would bring in crackers every morning when they came in to check on Nick.

'I would feel the nausea until about noon every day and then be all right until the next morning. One night while Nick was in the hospital, John wanted to take me to a concert that was in town. I imagine he felt I needed to get a break from all the stress related to Nick being in the hospital. I reluctantly agreed to go, under the condition that my mother was able to stay with Nick while we were gone, as I did not want Nick to be there alone. My mother was able to stay with Nick so we went. The entire time we were gone I felt so guilty that I had left my baby at the hospital, to go out to have fun. I felt that I was a horrible mother for this. About halfway through the concert, I could no longer take it. At that point, I broke down and started crying. I wanted to go back to the hospital to be with my baby.

'On 8 November 1997 Nick had corrective surgery for his reflux condition. John spent the day at work, leaving me to sit there and wait with my mother until Nick was out of surgery. When they came to take Nick, I had a difficult time letting him go. Fortunately my mother was there to hold my hand. They took

Nick and his favourite bear to surgery together. My mother spent most of the time Nick was in surgery watching me pace the floor. When they took Nick to the recovery room, the surgeon came in to tell us how everything went.

'He told us all had gone well and what we should expect when they brought Nick back to the room. They had placed a tube in his stomach to allow for feeding and burping if necessary. When they brought Nick to the room the nurses placed him in my arms while they took his vitals. Nick spent most of the rest of that day rocking in my arms and sleeping. He did not fuss much at all and the nurses said that was uncommon. John showed up late that afternoon to check on us and allowed me to take a break so that I could eat and stretch my legs.

'The next morning it was like I had my old Nick back. He was standing up in his crib, bouncing around, playing and laughing. I did not think much of it until the doctors and nurses said they had never seen anything like it before. Because of the way he was acting they decided that evening they would allow him to start back on liquids. Also that evening Nick discovered the tube they had placed in his abdomen. To Nick this was a built-in toy placed there just for him. I could not believe that a child would grab hold of that tube and yank on it the way he did. As he did this he would squeal with delight at himself. Within three days after the surgery they decided Nick was having entirely too much fun in the hospital, and even though the average time in the hospital was between one and two weeks after that surgery, they sent him home.

'Before we left, the hospital staff gave us tons of information. We were trained in infant and child CPR and were given a new diet for Nick to try to get him to gain weight and catch up to the babies his age. I was also trained on how to care for the skin around the tube in Nick's belly.

'When I got home with Nick my entire routine changed. I felt I had a chemistry lab in my kitchen just to make Nick's bottles. Then I felt that we also had a small clinic going to change the dressing around Nick's stomach tube. I also decided it might be best to make sure that Nick only wore one-piece outfits. I did this more to keep him from yanking on the tube than to hide it from people that might see it.

'For the first month after we returned home, I was constantly taking Nick back and forth to the doctors and we also had a couple of emergency room visits. He had to be readmitted at the end of November for a few days due to some complications with his recovery. Other than that, the visits to the hospital were because the child kept pulling the tube out of his stomach playing with it. I am not sure how many times we went to the hospital for this. However, I finally questioned his need for the tube with the surgeon and we decided to leave it out. I am not sure how much Nick missed his built-in toy, but I was so glad not to have to deal with it any more.

'What with all the equipment we had for Nick and the house being cramped, John and I decided that it was time to leave the little one-bedroom apartment that had been our love nest and try to get a bigger home.

'It took us a few months to find somewhere that we both liked. By the time we got everything moved in and the house the way we liked it, it was almost Christmas and it turned out that Santa was bringing a few surprises that year.

'Once we had been sorted in terms of the move, I got in touch with a paediatrician for Nick and found out that I was once again pregnant. With all the changes in my life and the problems with Nick I felt that I could not handle the prospect of a new baby. I must have cried about it for hours. John suggested that I have an abortion. That was out of the question – I could never have an abortion. I'm not exactly pro-life but I do not go along with the pro-choice ideals either. I've always thought of babies as a gift that we are given and we should value them. I loved this baby from the first moment I found out that I was pregnant but I was terribly worried about how I would manage and the fact that it too could have problems.

'We had a good next month or so before I started having

trouble with the pregnancy. The first thing to happen was that I got sick with a bout of pneumonia. John came home one afternoon to find me on the couch burning up with a fever. He immediately called the doctor and made arrangements for me to see her the next morning. She put me on antibiotics and watched me closely to make sure that the fever did not return to such a high level. Fortunately I responded rapidly to the antibiotics and there was no more concern for the baby or myself.

'As we were heading into February, I started having the same pains that I had with the pregnancy with Nick, except this time they were much sharper and much more frequent. I described them to the doctor and she expressed a concern that they were maybe pre-term labour pains but did not act as if she was as convinced as the other doctors had been that that was the case. She put me on bed rest and increased the frequency of my appointments to monitor me more closely.

'Because I had to spend most of the time in bed we had to put Nick in day care, which John complained greatly about as he usually would be the one taking him to and from the centre. He also had a way of pointing out the cost of it over and over and over to me. While on bed rest I did everything in my power to keep as busy as possible. I made many things for the babies (Nick and the one I was carrying). After a few weeks I truly thought that I would not be able to handle not being able to get up and do things. John also was not helping my morale at this point either; he was constantly letting me know that if he had married someone else this would not be happening. He went to great lengths to let me and everyone else know all the sacrifices he was making because of the situation. He could not go out after work with the guys and he could not continue to bowl in the bowling league because he had to be home to take care of Nick and me. He had changed so much from the man I had married, still being polite and kind in front of others but deriding me for ruining his life when we were alone. He told me that he still loved me and Nick, but that at times he wished he had married someone else.

'He made me feel so guilty that I would try to get up and clean and also cook as much as possible. Most of the time I did this I paid dearly for it because I would more than likely be in severe pain for several hours afterwards. He never seemed to care that I was in pain, he just cared that he could no longer do what he wanted to do.

'I continued this way until June 1998. John and I were to go out for dinner that evening. I was at home alone when everything started to go seriously wrong with my health. I had just eaten some lunch and was lying in bed watching television. Suddenly, I was struck with such an immense pain that I immediately doubled over in agony.

'It was more intense than anything I had experienced in the past and it would not let up as it had done before. After a short amount of time the pain started to make me very nauseous. I struggled greatly to make it into the bathroom. I was sicker than I had ever been in my life. I could barely move from the pain. It wasn't long before I became convinced that I would not survive whatever it was that was happening to me at the time. I was exhausted from the excruciating pain and nausea. I barely had any strength when I thought about the baby I was carrying. I had to do everything I could to try to get help for both of us.

'If it were just me, I may have given up at that moment. Thinking of my unborn child, however, caused me to panic. I crawled back into the bedroom to get the phone. When I finally got the phone, I immediately called the doctor, who was in surgery at the time. I told the nurse what was going on and she told me to hold on while she tried to reach the doctor. At that point I must have passed out for a short time.

'When I came back around the connection on the phone was lost. I then got a call back from the nurse, telling me to get to the hospital. At that point I could no longer think straight and also had no way of being able to get to the car. I am sure that whatever I was saying to anyone made no sense whatsoever. Through all of this no one thought to call 911 to get me some help. I tried to get up and find some strength to get to the hospital but passed out once again. I was startled about an hour later by the phone ringing. This time it was John. I told him what was happening. He left work immediately to come and get me.

'John arrived about 45 minutes to an hour later. He rushed me out the door and into the car. By that time the pains had subsided some — either that or I was getting used to them, I'm not sure which. I could however feel some peaks and valleys to the intensity of them. I also noticed that they were somewhat regular. About the time I noticed this, the car ran out of gas! I could not believe this! Now I was in great pain, sure that I was in pre-term labour and parked on the side of a road out of gas. What more was going to happen that day?

'John then admitted he knew that he had been low on gas but wanted to get to me as soon as possible and then get gas later. At that point I was sure that I was married to the biggest idiot in the world. I realise most guys like to see exactly how far they can drive before having to refill the tank but this time it was playing with lives that were not his own. Did I want to rip his face off at that point? Yes, and if I did not need him so much at the time to get me to the hospital I may have tried it.

'When we finally reached the hospital, I had him stop at the door to let me out. I grabbed my pillow, got out, slammed the door to the car and walked in, mumbling to myself. I walked up to the nurses, who were awaiting my arrival. After finding out what was up they decided it best to keep John away from me until I had a chance to calm down some. They had me change and hooked me up to some monitors to measure the contractions. They checked on me frequently until the doctor arrived. She ordered some tests and asked why it took so long to get to the hospital. I told her what had happened. Her advice was to call 911 next time. They sent me for an ultrasound, which at first I thought was to check the baby. I was wrong – they were checking my gall bladder. The technician said she had never seen a gall bladder so full of stones. No wonder I was having so much pain for so long.

'When they got me back to labour and delivery the doctor told me that I did indeed have gallstones as she had suspected and she was calling in another doctor for me to see.

'When the surgeon arrived he explained how bad the situation was and told me I was to be admitted. He also explained that this had apparently been going on for some time and he could not understand why it had taken so long to diagnose.

'John explained that I had been telling the doctors what was going on with me but they seemed to be dismissing it. The doctor asked many questions trying to determine what would have set off such a severe attack. After going through what I had eaten that day and the day before and what I had done activity-wise, he decided that the attack was spontaneous, coming on without any specific cause.

'The doctors decided at that time that the gall bladder had to be removed, but the question was when. If they were to take the gall bladder at that point they would also have to take the baby. The baby was not far enough along to be born without severe complications, so it was decided to monitor the situation and keep me at the hospital. By this time the pain had subsided enough that I was starting to realise that I was very hungry. The doctors decided it would be best if I did not eat anything at that point. Little did I know this was soon to become a trend.

'After they moved me to a room and got me settled in they came in and gave me something for the pain. It only took them eight hours. As much as I hate needles, after the day I'd had, the thought of some relief was very welcome. They put the pain medication in my IV and it took effect immediately. I was asleep in no time.

'The next day they started me on a regimen of antibiotics, medication for pre-term labour and pain medications. I worried about all the medication with the baby but the doctors said it was necessary. They told me that what was most important at the time was to keep the baby from being born as long as possible, as they felt he would not be able to breathe on his own at that point. The medications they had me on totally confused my system. The medication to prevent pre-term labour acted as a stimulant, so I was edgy, nervous and constantly hot. I could not get the room cool enough for my liking. However the nurses all swore they needed to invest in parkas in order to be able to come into my room. Of course the pain medication acted as a depressant and that is what served to confuse my body, as it didn't know if I should be hyper or laidback. It wound up that I was constantly miserable to be around.

'I missed Nick terribly during this time. John would bring him in as often as possible to see me. Nick would climb all over the bed, so excited he could hardly contain himself. And the IV lines were in his mind a new toy, which made things very interesting. I was surprised that Nick did not seem to mind the hospital. I felt he might not feel comfortable in there even though it was not the same one he had been in. He was always very upbeat when he came to visit.

'Most of the three weeks I was in the hospital before they decided it was time to take the baby I was not able to eat. I could no longer hold down any foods or liquids. They started IV nutritional supplements. The fats that they were giving me caused my veins to go bad very quickly. Almost every morning they would have to come in and change the location of the IV. This was sheer torture for me as I have always hated needles and my veins were very quickly shot by these procedures. During the last week before they delivered the baby I was extremely nauseated, even though I was not eating or drinking anything.

'They started giving me yet another medication that helped to control the nausea for a few days longer, until it came to the point that nothing helped. Then they kept taking me in to do a test to see if the baby's lungs were developed enough that he could breathe.

'It was during these tests that someone let slip I was having another boy, taking the fun out of that part of the birth. The test showed that his lungs were developed. They immediately began making arrangements to deliver the baby and get my gall bladder out. I initially thought they were going to do surgery to remove my gall bladder and at that point I would wake up from surgery in labour. They then told me that they had to deliver the baby first, as the surgeon would not be able to reach the gall bladder because the baby had grown so much.

'I was pretty much all right with whatever they chose to do because I just wanted it all over and I wanted to go home. I also wanted very badly to eat again.

'On the morning of the operation, the doctors came in to tell me what to expect from the surgery they were going to do. They told me they planned to take the baby first and they would allow me to be awake for that. Then they planned on putting me to sleep to remove my gall bladder. This was also the point that they told me they expected the baby to be born addicted to the pain medication that I had been on.

'Needless to say I practically lost it at that point. I was so angry with them for not telling me about this beforehand. I cannot say now if I would have been able to totally do without the pain medication, but I definitely would have tried. I felt so much guilt at that point. All I could think of was the crack-addicted babies that I had seen in the past. I was terrified my baby would be like that.

'It was not long before they had the baby out. When they had him out everyone immediately moved to the side of the room that they had taken the baby to. I did not hear any crying so I was very upset. I kept asking if he was breathing but no one would answer. I started to fight the restraints and started demanding that someone tell me if my baby was OK. Still no one would answer me.

'After I started to struggle more desperately the anaesthesiologist stood up and demanded someone answer me before I got out of the restraints to find out for myself. They finally answered and let me know that he was indeed breathing. After a bit they brought him over to me. John held him close to me and unrestrained one of my arms so that I could touch him. I wanted more time with him but it was not long before the second surgical team was ready to go. John took the baby back to the neonatologist, as the anaesthesiologist told me goodnight.

'I woke up in recovery, immediately wanting to know how my baby was doing. I was still very groggy from the anaesthesia when the nurses started to update me on the baby's status. They were very cheerful and bubbly. It seemed they had all gone to the nursery to see him. They told me he was the first baby born in the regular OR [operating room] at that hospital. They went on and on about how precious he was and how well he was doing.

'Their cheerfulness started to get to me, as I was still very sedated. I tried to go back to sleep to no avail as they continued waking me up. About 5.30 or 6 pm they took me back to my room, which was a new room. The nurses had ordered me a private room. They said they felt that I did not need all the commotion that a regular room on the maternity floor has and also I would be able to have the baby with me more if I was in a private room. My mother and John were both still at the hospital. They told me that it was at least an hour or more before the staff would allow them to be with Luke (the baby). They had to put him on oxygen for about an hour because he was not getting enough at first but everything was OK. After my mother and John left the nurses brought Luke to me from the nursery. I must have spent hours holding him and talking to him. He lay in my arms and intently looked at me as I talked to him. He seemed so alert to me, especially considering that he was premature. Of course you would not know it to look at him; he weighed in at 6 lb 8 oz. I was told there were full-term babies in the nursery that weighed less.

'Luke was not home for much more than a week before he had to be readmitted to the hospital and more tests done on him. I first noticed that he was having more bowel movements than normal and they also had a strange odour. This was the first sign of something being wrong. When he was in the hospital, the doctor discovered that Luke had a malabsorption problem. He was not able to break down the fats in the formula or my breast milk.

'Unfortunately, it soon became apparent that baby Luke had some of the same problems as Nick and breaking down milk fats would be the least of his problems. One day in the middle of August I was working in the kitchen after I had laid Luke down for his nap. Nick was still awake and playing around the house. About the time I realised that Nick was missing from the kitchen, I heard him making a terrible racket in Luke's room. He was screaming at the top of his lungs and as I got closer to Luke's room I could hear that Nick was shaking Luke's crib viciously. At first I was very upset that Nick would go into Luke's room and disturb him when he was sleeping, as he had never done this before.

'When I went into Luke's room I immediately saw that Luke had turned an ashen shade of grey. I immediately scooped him up into my arms, calling out his name. I rubbed his body vigorously, trying to get a response from him but got nothing at all. His little body was totally limp. As I was walking into the bathroom with him I felt to see if I could feel a pulse as I had been instructed to do in the past. I felt a very weak pulse but it was very slow. I laid him down on the counter in the bathroom and started CPR.

'When Luke started to make an effort to breathe again on his own he started to spit up mucus. I had never seen him do this before. I wanted to call for an ambulance but at that moment Luke was spitting up so much mucus and crying so hard that I was afraid to divert my attention from him to get the phone. After a short time he slowed down on spitting up the mucus enough that I felt I could call for some help, which I did. It took very little time for the paramedics to arrive.

'When they did, Luke's colour was still very poor, so they did not waste much time getting him ready to take to the hospital. I asked if they felt it would be OK to take him to the children's hospital that he normally went to as they had all of his records there. They told me that they would try but they would go to the closest hospital if he had another episode. Since I had Nick with me I could not ride in the ambulance with Luke so I decided to follow with Nick in the car.

'When Nick and I arrived at the hospital, they already had Luke in an exam room in the ER. He seemed a little bit more settled. I asked the paramedics what had happened on the road that they had taken off so quickly. One of them told me that Luke started to make some choking noises and they just didn't want to waste any time. In case something happened they would have preferred to be at the hospital instead of on the road. He then told me that nothing more came of it other than he spat up some more mucus.

'It wasn't long before my mother and John arrived at the ER. Not long after their arrival the doctor that was treating Luke ordered a test that required some of the mucus that Luke had been spitting up. When the results from the test came back the doctor told us that Luke had a virus called RSV, which caused babies to have apnoeas. The reason for this is that children under one year of age could not cough up the mucus created in their systems fast enough to clear their airways. Therefore they would eventually not be able to breathe because their airways would be blocked from the mucus. The doctor told me that Luke would have to be admitted yet again. After they had Luke settled in his room, John decided to take Nick home and call me when he had Nick fed and settled in for the evening. One of the specialists that saw Luke ordered that he be put back on the apnoea monitor and started on whatever treatment was needed to handle the symptoms of the RSV virus.

'The nurses gave me more information about the virus Luke had contracted and what to expect. The next day Luke developed a high temperature and also started to develop the symptoms that he had when he was having problems breaking down the fats in his feed. It was very hard for me to watch how bad he was doing. He lay in his crib almost lifeless in my eyes. I could not get him to eat or respond to me unless he was coughing up mucus after his breathing treatments.

'The doctors started questioning me once again about his apnoeas and what exactly had happened that led up to Luke being brought into the hospital. They showed a good deal of displeasure when I could not tell them exactly how long he was not breathing. No matter how many times I told them I was not present in the room when he stopped breathing, so there was no way I could tell them how long he wasn't breathing, they persisted that I tell them an approximate time. They also wanted to hear over and over what I had to do to intervene to get him to start breathing again. One doctor went so far as to question my perceptions of what had happened.

'I tried to keep calm as I didn't want Luke to pick up on the fact that I was so worried. That night I kept waking up from dreams in which I was holding Luke's lifeless body. I could not get over the feeling that my baby was cold. I was wrapping him up in blankets and no matter what anybody said I would not let go of him.

'The next day the surgeon came in and spoke to me about what he saw. He said there was no need to do any surgery on Luke, that the X-ray had been improperly read. I was so happy I hugged him. Even though the threat of surgery was over I still had those dreams for a very long time.

'In October of that year, the doctors admitted Luke to run some more tests on him, as his apnoeas had become so prevalent. One of the tests that they ran was a sleep study; this study showed a correlation between his reflux and his apnoeas. The pulmonologist explained that this was very dangerous and that they were recommending surgery like Nick had had to correct the problem. I told him that I wanted to speak with the surgeon to confirm what the tests had shown and get his feelings on the surgery first. This was done later that day.

'After speaking to the surgeon I was comfortable with the idea that this would be the best course of action for Luke's well being. I still had a hard time understanding how it was that Luke could be thriving and still be in the type of danger that the doctors had explained he was in.

'I told John what the doctors had recommended and when they wanted to do the surgery. He was in agreement that this should be done. Even though I trusted the doctors' opinion and would agree that the surgery was prudent, I had a slight feeling of dread about the procedure.

'I was willing to accept doing anything to be able to have a healthy child. Nick was doing so well at that point despite his small size, which I heard concerns about constantly from the doctors. I also had many people asking me if he was premature and was that why he was so small. It had gotten to the point I wanted to lie about Nick's age in order to avoid the constant questions from well-meaning people. I hated feeling this way but I wanted so badly to have children that everyone accepted as normal and not different. It is hard to explain how difficult it is for a mother that has fought so hard to do what is best for her children to constantly be bombarded with questions about why her child is different.

'I also did not want either Nick or Luke to pick up on what type of attention was being bestowed upon them. I felt that it could be detrimental for their self-esteem to pick up on how people responded to a child that had problems.

'About this time I was also getting slack from John. He was starting to tell me almost constantly that if I were not in his life, his life would be so much better. He would blame me for the children's medical problems as if his genes played no contributing factor in their problems and only mine could have.

'During the summer both Nick and Luke continued to improve developmentally. Nick remained very small for his age and Luke continued to have apnoeas. We had both of the boys on special diets – Nick was on pediasure in order to try to gain weight and Luke was on the predigested formula. By the end of the summer Luke was also eating cereals and some baby foods. Luke, unlike Nick, was gaining weight by leaps and bounds. It was hard for me to imagine that Luke had all the medical problems that he did have, since he looked so healthy.

'A few months later, Luke was back in hospital. He had developed a questionable pneumonia. I asked the doctors if this would be a condition that Luke would be bothered with long term since he was premature. I had an older sister who had two premature daughters who had constant problems with pneumonia. The pulmonologist felt it would be best not to worry about that at that point since Luke had not had significant problems with that so far and he was getting along pretty well despite his rough start.

'He did at that time diagnose Luke with reactive airway disease, which was explained to me as a form of asthma, which the doctors felt was due to Luke's being born prematurely.

'He also explained that he did not want to officially diagnose asthma for insurance purposes and also it would trigger more tests for Luke that would not change the way they treated him for the symptoms.

'Before we left the hospital that time, we were provided with a piece of equipment that would allow John and I to give Luke breathing treatments at home. This was like giving him a prescription inhaler like an older person would use, except since Luke was so young he could not use an inhaler so the machine would administer the medication to him in a vapour, which he could breathe in more slowly and easily.

'Luke would take the treatments very easily and seemed to enjoy chewing on the end of the tube that the vapour came out of. The nurses that would come out to our home to download his monitor would also help to maintain the breathing machine and provide us with the medication and equipment necessary to give Luke his treatments.

'During this time once a month a nurse would come out to our home to download the monitor that Luke would sleep with. The monitor would record any events of apnoea and/or low or high heart rates. The nurse would have the monitor company send me the printouts from the monitor every month.

'The nurse told me that the monitor printouts were also being sent to the doctors that cared for Luke.

'That November, the company that John worked for changed

insurance coverage for health care. This involved changing the boys' paediatrician, but not the specialists that they saw. I was not overly thrilled with this.

'It was not many months after the change in insurance coverage that Luke was due to go in for his six-month check-up. When I met with the doctor for the first time I explained the problems that the boys had and what specialists were following their care. She seemed to be pleased with the doctors that the boys had and made notes in their charts to provide referrals for them to see the specialists when required follow-up appointments were necessary. We also discussed Luke being on the apnoea monitor.

'Things with the boys' health seemed to be going fine for a while. During the month of February, the doctor decided that Luke no longer needed his monitor. I was obviously nervous about the decision to take him off the monitor, but I convinced myself that I was using it as a crutch. At first it was very hard for me to sleep comfortably but I eventually got used to the idea that he might have actually outgrown the need for it. It was easier to not have to keep up with putting Luke on the monitor every time he was put to sleep.

'Things seemed to have turned the corner by that point and we were contemplating having a normal family life, when John and I were called into a meeting at the hospital. We had been arguing a lot in front of the children and medical staff and we assumed it was to do with that, but we were wrong.

'We met in a conference room at the hospital. At the meeting we were told that the doctors had concerns that I was maybe causing Luke's problems and we would be contacted by Child Protection Services. The doctors made it sound like it was more of a formality than anything else. We were not happy about the news but after hearing from our doctor that he truly felt that I had nothing to do with Luke's problems we were not overly concerned.

'I thought the entire idea was very strange – that we would need to be investigated for trying to get the medical care that my child needed. I was always under the impression that people were investigated for not taking their kids to the doctor when they were sick.

'I was not paying too much attention to this because John and I had decided to split. It was not just because he felt I was a weight on his life, holding him back. He also complained that I never made him feel like a real husband and I spent all my time worrying about the children instead of finding a balance to give him some attention.

'So you can imagine the perfect family that was discovered by Child Protection Services. They told me that they had been contacted with concerns that I was making Luke sick and they also believed that no one other than myself had seen Luke's apnoeas.

'The officer in charge requested I give him a list of everyone that had witnessed the apnoea episodes. He was surprised to learn that I was not only able to give him a list of people but also copies of the monitor downloads.

'I quickly learned that they were trying to build a case against me and never looked at the evidence supporting the truth that I was doing nothing to my child other than to try to get him the help that he needed. After a few visits I was informed that I was accused of having a mental disorder called Munchausen's Syndrome by Proxy.

'I was given some information on the so-called disorder and also given a profile that had been developed to determine who could have the disorder. When I read the profile I quickly noticed that 99 per cent of mothers could easily fit it, as it was very vague and in part relied on medical assumptions, not medical fact. The thought that you could easily fit anyone into the profile they were using scared me very much, as I could see no way of defending myself against it. If you say that no, you are not a good mother, they got you on that. If you deny the accusation, you fit the profile. If you are of above average intelligence and have some medical knowledge you are pretty much sunk.

'I started to research the condition and discovered support

groups on the Internet. Unfortunately, while supportive, the Web sites were never optimistic. Once accused, women seemed to lose their children. I posted under a variety of names to the Web sites and Internet lists as I had heard that the authorities also looked at these places.

'It was at this point that I was informed my complete medical background was being looked into. At a meeting in January 2000, it was put to me by one of the psychologists present that most of the incidents involving the children were witnessed by very few people except me. They also raised the back and leg pain from 1996, saying they knew incidents had happened but had I played up on them to get attention for myself?

'When I asked them why I would do this, they told me that it may have been a subconscious cry for help or doubts about the marriage. When I pointed out to them that at that time John and I were getting on fine, they resorted to talking about the subconscious again, saying that I might have thought things were fine, but perhaps deep down I knew they weren't and that was why I was behaving that way, as a cry for help. I couldn't win.

'They also told me that the postings to the Internet, which I had told them about, under multiple names may be some sign of other mental illness. They could not get it into their heads that I was doing it to protect my anonymity and also to make sure no one could identify me. They thought using other names was a sure sign of having something to hide.

'I denied the allegations and told them that if they insisted I no longer take Luke to the hospital when I felt he needed treatment I would hold them responsible for any negative outcome with Luke. At that point I was told to take Luke to the hospital if I ever felt he needed to be seen. I told them that I felt if I did it would be used against me.

'John and I got back together around this time, as he said that while we were not perfect, he realised the children were also his and he had a responsibility not only to them, but also to me. One of the few times he has acted like the Southern gentleman that you always read about.

'The Child Protection Services continued to make unannounced visits to our home to check up on me. They would tell me over and over again that the state wanted to help me. Of course, I would reply that I did not want their help as I did not trust their motives in my situation.

'As time went by the visits became fewer and fewer, especially after John moved back in.

'Then one day the boys got into the medicine cabinet and got hold of a prescription that contained opium as an ingredient. They at most could have only gotten hold of two pills. I still called the paediatrician's office and asked them what to do about the boys possibly taking this medicine. I told them I was not sure if they took the pills and if they had it was only two at most. At first the nurse said there was nothing to worry about. After a bit she called me back and said that the doctor had instructed her to tell me to take the kids to the hospital.

'I took the boys into the hospital and there the doctor ordered their stomachs pumped and had them admitted for observation overnight. They put the boys in two different rooms. I spent most of the night running between the two rooms.

'After that, the visits from the department increased and I was told that a full-blown investigation into my past and the boys' medical past, most of which you've read here, was being instigated to see if I had been abusing the boys from their earliest days.

'They eventually told us that they would leave us alone if we would agree to put the boys into day care while John was away at work. We told them we would agree as long as they paid for the day care and we got to choose it. They baulked at it at first but eventually they agreed because we argued there was no need for the boys to be in day care, as they had a mother fully capable of taking care of them at home.

'Then we were told that the boys were to be taken off us as a precautionary measure. We argued against this and pleaded, but in their eyes I was a bad parent. The boys were taken away from me in January 2001. They spent just over a week in a care home before being given to foster parents, who have them to this day. We have no visiting rights, though John has been told that he can visit without me. I've been told that the case against me is still being investigated. No charges have been brought against me but the social workers are continuing to try to build a case. I'm not altogether optimistic but I have to try. What mother wouldn't?

Eight

The Argument Against MSBP

MSBP is a fairly modern condition, having been discovered in the late 1970s. There may then be some irony in the fact that for the first 10 to 15 years of its existence, those who were accused of it or those who did not believe it existed were unable to mount a proper cohesive defence against the condition.

People who made the newspapers after being accused of it were occasionally contacted by others like them and small support groups were set up that way, but there was no unified approach to the topic or the problem.

Until the Internet came along. The Internet helped in many ways. First, it served as an online library where accused people could go to learn more about the syndrome that could land them in jail or have their children taken away from them.

Second, it let them see how others had countered and fought the allegations, giving them hope in fighting their own cases.

Third, it allowed people to set up forums where they could get in touch with each other, forming online support groups.

Lastly, it gave them a place to air their grievances, away from the possible censorship, legal problems or lack of interest that they might have found in other media outlets. With the arrival of the World Wide Web, the accused suddenly become empowered and they could fight back.

MSBP started in Britain and three of the most prolific campaigners against it there are Penny Mellor, Brian Morgan and

Bobbie Isbell.

Penny has set up a group, Dare to Care, to help parents. It has helped more than 50 families who say they were wrongly accused, and the vast majority – more than 90 per cent – have been cleared of the accusations.

She believes that children can be taken away because they display problems that could have been caused by other factors, such as an adverse reaction to drugs or routine vaccinations.

In her words: 'This is nothing more than a form of legalised kidnapping. It devastates the lives of parents and the children it seeks to protect, who are often put into a loveless and sometimes abusive care system that churns out dysfunctional adults, which benefits no one.'

A freelance journalist from Cardiff, Brian Morgan, 60, has spent the last seven years working on medical negligence cases throughout Britain. He has criticised Professor David Southall's methods.

Morgan has had his home raided by police, with them removing files and computer equipment and has also been criticised in the press by fellow journalists. A 1999 press release by the British Medical Association, issued on behalf of Professor Southall, accused Morgan of 'an orchestrated campaign to obstruct child protection work'. Morgan denied this and said he would be seeking legal representation over the claims.

Morgan was one of the first to draw parallels between MSBP and the Cleveland, England scandal in the 1980s, when more than 100 children were taken from their homes on the basis of a diagnostic technique that was later dismissed and discredited.

He believes that parents are being accused of a new form of child abuse. In his eyes: 'There is no medical consensus and it is being used without any proper evaluation.'

Brian's work started in the early nineties when he learnt of an MSBP-related gagging order taken out against the *Cambrian News*, a Welsh newspaper based in Aberystwyth. He later worked on a documentary about MSBP, which was shown on the British TV programme *Dispatches*.

As he has pointed out in his article *A Study in Secrecy*, which is one of the most widely read documents on MSBP on the Internet: 'After the *Dispatches* research was complete, evidence continued to accumulate that a small number of medical experts, with the willing co-operation of the legal and social work professions, have used the secrecy of the children's legal protection process to promote, internationally, a new child abuse diagnosis.

'This has echoes from Cleveland, where child abuse investigators were relying upon evidence of "anal dilatation" before it had become generally accepted as a valid diagnostic tool. Respectability for this technique was never achieved and its use was abandoned.

'The comparison has been made with Cleveland and the witchcraft trials [of the Middle Ages] and it's quite sad to notice that in some ways nothing has changed. In those days you had Witchfinder Generals who led the accusations and nowadays we have some doctors leading the accusations.

'I'm a science writer and the fact that it is scientific evidence is another reason I got involved. There is no scientific credibility to it.

'Now parents are being falsely accused of a new form of child abuse. In order to maintain their credibility and (dare one say, without risk of legal action) the high fees they can earn as "experts", the medical profession repeatedly denies there are any false allegations, despite well-researched and clear documentation to the contrary.'

Morgan is intelligent enough to know that children may be being abused by their parents. What worries him is the tag of MSBP and the culture of secrecy that surrounds it.

'I do not believe that all families accused of MSBP who turn to the media for help are entirely innocent of some kind of inappropriate parenting – even if the MSBP label is being abused. In the same way, whilst comparing the MSBP diagnosis with anal dilatation in Cleveland (the comparison is with the lack of scientific validation, not with the absence of any abuse – some children were being sexually abused in Cleveland, it was the way the diagnosis was used that completely screwed up the management of cases), some abused children went back to abusive homes and some were abused in care by other abused children.'

Morgan feels that two of the biggest dangers are the secretive nature of the cases, which take place in the family courts, and the way evidence is presented in court.

'A mother may stand accused of having a mental illness – which is not officially recognised – without the accusers having any forensic evidence to back the allegations being made.

'And there is no information currently available as to whether the authorities even remotely consider what safeguards need to be put in place to avoid the scenario of innocent mothers falsely confessing to abuse under officially sanctioned blackmail to avoid losing their children.'

Further proof of the problems in diagnosing people with MSBP, in Morgan's eyes, are the checklists compiled to identify MSBP sufferers.

'There are a dozen or so "features" like these that could apply to large numbers of people, which implies that a small but significant proportion of the population could be open to accusations that they suffer from MSBP, were allegations of abuse ever laid at their door.

'MSBP is very self-perpetuating as the same people keep appearing as experts, but where are the students carrying the torch of MSBP? There are none.

'MSBP is in many ways a diagnosis that can be lazy at times, but even worse, at times it is used to cover up accidental harm to the child. There are many who will not just admit that they do not know what is up.'

Another problem involving secrecy is the way the press are dealt with, not only with regard to reporting MSBP court cases, but also in general attempts at getting information involving accusations of child abuse or MSBP.

'It is not unheard of for injunctions which prevent the family involved even talking to the press, or the press reporting any information which may have been researched elsewhere, to protect the professionals, particularly from medicine and social work, from scrutiny.

'Organisations suspecting that a particular person has been leaked documents can, and have, without any evidence that that person has received them, obtain injunctions as part of a "fishing expedition" to prevent use of the information contained in them. This happened to me initially and I had to rely upon the National Union of Journalists to step in and defend my position.

'Being investigated and having equipment taken has made me a lot poorer, especially when stories you are researching get gagged and you can't get anything printed, and then paid for, despite the hours, days and weeks of effort you may have put into it.'

But he feels the press could do more to shed light on the situation.

'The press – the tabloids especially – have a tendency to lose interest in a story if the child and family involved cannot be named, which is often the case if a legal order has been taken out. It is less of a problem for the broadsheets, which tend to balance the public interest in exposing an underlying scandal against the lack of an identifiable family. But sadly it is the tabloid press rather than the broadsheets that have the resources for investigations – and they will not investigate false allegation cases, however strong, where the mother cannot be named. The same goes for the great and admirable "injustice" strands on television.

'The legal threats – and the courts' willingness to impose gagging orders – are two of the major problems in getting things into the public forum. No one refuses a gagging order when it appears that children's safety is at risk.

'I always remember an editor telling me that it was the courts covering up for the professionals and that is what it has been at times.

'For lawyers the whole process can be very lucrative as you can have huge teams involved in cases lasting for weeks. So there is also a lot of money at stake as well as reputations.'

Seeking publicity can also be used against the family fighting the MSBP accusations, according to Morgan.

'One of the myths promoted by the doctors who believe in MSBP is that seeking publicity is a characteristic of the MSBP abuser and that can be a strong enough deterrent to put someone off seeking the help of the media to prove their innocence. It can also explain why lawyers are reluctant to allow the families to expose themselves to possible publicity – if for no other reason than to do so might be taken to imply guilt.'

Morgan also has advice for those looking to work with those accused of MSBP and fight the allegations: 'Statutory complaints procedures can be used very effectively to force information out of social services departments' files, hospitals and health authorities. This can be a protracted process and is usually a waiting game – for some particularly revealing information to emerge to be fitted jigsaw-like into data from another case, possibly even in a different country.

'Journalists may need to help families draft letters of complaint and point them in the direction of the appropriate complaints procedures for different institutions. In my opinion this is an entirely ethical approach, justifiable in the public interest and necessary in view of the willingness of the courts to grant unlimited injunctions on an ex parte [one-sided] basis without pausing to consider the alternatives – time limitation, for example, or reporting restrictions.

'For parents with access to the Internet, that has been a useful ally, but many still do not have access to it.

'For the press, it is essential that journalists should work with the family without disclosing media involvement. The merest hint of press interest in a case leads the local authority or hospital involved to take out an ex parte injunction.'

Bobbie Isbell has taken a wider view of the problem of MSBP than some of the other campaigners in this chapter, having lived in America and Britain. She has been campaigning for years about family and child rights in both countries, becoming involved through a high-profile Shaken Baby Syndrome (SBS) case as a researcher.

'As I uncovered more cases of wrongful accusations of child abuse by SBS, I found other areas such as SIDS (Sudden Infant

Death Syndrome) and MSBP being used as a means for taking children into care or to prosecute the innocent.

'This for me set alarm bells ringing, for at the time of this high profile case, I had experienced four years of foster parenting, and was still attempting to right the wrongs done to children in care in my locality.

'I experienced firsthand how unprofessional care within social services is, and how this incompetence can cause more harm to families and consequently to the children. The term bandied about by some in social services, "in the best interests of the child", is nothing more than words to them. In my opinion, the term is used in a flippant and superior manner to stroke egos and to appear "all knowing".

'MSBP, by its very wide diagnosis and evaluation process, is unsafe. Even the "experts" argue over the controversial diagnosis.

'Being an American living in the UK, I have noticed the increased usage of this term in the UK during the last decade. I always say, "What happens in the US buys a ticket, gets the flight, and finally comes over here", though MSBP would appear to have done the opposite.

'Anything with the suffix "syndrome" is troublesome. The word "syndrome" simply relates to a deduction based on a set of symptoms, and is not a diagnosis. Many mental and physical illnesses mimic other illnesses and have similar "symptoms".

'To say that every individual has the same symptoms, and then use that as the basis of a diagnosis for use in a court of law, is dangerous indeed. It is a very telling fact that MSBP is not recognised by either the American Medical Association or the American Psychiatric Association, and if any so-called expert in the field of MSBP tries to tell people otherwise, they are misleading them.

'A diagnosis of MSBP involves identifying the psychological motivation of the parent. The evaluation is usually done during a time of family crisis – perhaps when a child who has been ill for a long time is critically ill or dying – a time when even the most experienced psychologist would hesitate to attempt an accurate assessment.

'Yet we have doctors, paediatricians and yes, even psychologists doing these evaluations at a time when any parent would most certainly be exhibiting signs of high emotional distress. We also have some in Social Services validating these claims, despite their lack of knowledge or experience.

'This is why the combination of evaluation and diagnosis can bring about an allegation – an allegation that is usually unwarranted 9 times out of 10.'

Unlike many others though, Bobbie believes there is such a thing as MSBP – it's the frequency of cases that she has problems with.

'Genuine MSBP is rare. However, certain areas of the medical and child profession are hell-bent on making it more common. Why should any professional do such a thing? The old reasons of power and money.

'With consultation fees in this field being £2,000 for the one-hour assessment, I would say an evaluator of MSBP is highly motivated to find the result that benefits the budget requirements of the participating social service or hospital authority.

'One does not have to be reminded how the Orkney and Cleveland Reports show the over-zealousness of participating medical practitioners to realise that we are currently experiencing a revival, albeit with a different name, of a type of open season witch-hunt on parents who simply demand more information from doctors in respect of their child's illness.

'With the Internet explosion, parents are becoming more medically knowledgeable. Now they demand more information, complain more about the care, or lack of it, of their children. Unfortunately, the medical profession is, in the main, still arrogant enough to believe that it is infallible. Many of its members cannot bring themselves to contemplate the possibility that they do not have all the answers.

'MSBP and its diagnosis is going to get worse before it gets better. It is no exaggeration to say that every parent who is serious in advocating for their child is in imminent danger of this cruel and ridiculous allegation.

'Many parents have already suffered the wrongful allegations. Excellent mothers are emotionally raped, publicly slandered, criminally charged and jailed. Even if their child is eventually returned, they will suffer a lifetime from the trauma and maybe tens or hundreds of thousands of pounds or dollars in debt from the legal fees.

'As for the children, the false MSBP diagnosis can be gravely detrimental in that it adds deep emotional stress to an already ill child because of maternal deprivation. Aggressive treatment may be stopped with the assumption that just "removing the mother" will get results, risking serious consequences to the child's well being.

'The child's health is further jeopardised because the mother's watchful eye is replaced by rotating nurses who have little or no experience with the child and his or her idiosyncrasies. Relatives, friends and even family ministers are barred from nurturing or advocating for the child, branded as a threat and guilty by association.

'The child is held "medical hostage" under the care of a physician or hospital who might be prepared to do anything to protect their credibility.

'How will it end? Like all recent medical incompetence, MSBP will run full steam before a fighter for truth breaks down the barriers of this erroneous and unethical crusade mounted by those who propound MSBP. Penny Mellor is just such a fighter for truth and I believe she will be at the forefront of getting things changed.

'And if it ever gets to trial, then it will end with a sensational trial, where many heads will roll in order that family rights and justice can prevail against the numerous trumped-up charges of MSBP that there have been.'

Scotsman Stuart Carnie has provided help and support in some MSBP cases. He admits he is no expert on the matter, but worries about the lack of openness.

'First you have a small group of experts sticking to the theory. They rarely seem to attract more people to their cause or beliefs.

Indeed, most of the medical community seems to shy away from the topic, which is hardly a vote of confidence.

'You also have the whole issue of secrecy surrounding the situation, particularly when it comes to court cases and press reporting. We live in a so-called democracy with a free press, yet at the same time there seems to be a lack of freedom here. To make it even more draconian, there are situations where the press cannot even report on the fact that they are being gagged, which is absurd.

'Lastly, if those who believe in MSBP are so convinced of their theories and beliefs, why do they never debate the matter in public? The main way you hear of them is through medical journals or press releases.

'Now I'm not suggesting for one minute that these people have something to hide, but if they have enough confidence in their theories then they should stand up and defend them.

'That's what those who do not believe in MSBP have done. They have taken a public stance and done what has had to be done to get the matter into the public forum, using whatever tools they could. I once heard the phrase "conspiracy of silence" and that could almost apply here.'

Other countries on the Western side of the Atlantic have also helped to combat the claims of those who are for MSBP.

Tomas Ahlbeck in Sweden started a Web site, www.stop-abuse.de, to fight the sickening rise of child pornography on the Web. About a year into running the site, he was made aware of MSBP and he then started to use the site to counter that form of, as he perceived it, child abuse.

He said: 'MSBP became a part of my Web site in late 1998. I was contacted by Penny Mellor about a case of a young girl that involved allegations of MSBP.

'Penny did not know how to get attention to this, so I put up a page with some text and a picture. I then got more material from Penny and also others. We put up a tape recording of the girl on the Internet where she pleaded that the UK authorities would let her join her family.

'Then I got threats that things would happen to me if I did not close it down. That made me even more convinced that there must be some truth in the claims that MSBP was a fake diagnosis. Otherwise why would the authorities be so afraid that documents, audio evidence and other stuff should be published that they put out threats to someone who assisted in publishing it?

'It quickly became an important topic to the site and it is now responsible for about one-quarter of all the mail I receive as well as the information on the site itself. I now average over 400 visitors a day from all over the world, so there is a continual interest in it as well as there being a mailing list sent through e-mail on the matter.

'I did not know much at the beginning when I was first approached about it but now I have to say that I cannot see any reason why so many reporters, child rights activists and even people with a medical profession would lend their good name to the fight against alleged MSBP-accused if they did not have a reason to.

'I do not think that all mothers accused of MSBP are innocent of abusing their children, but I do not believe they are guilty of MSBP. Why? Because to me MSBP sounds like an invention from doctors to hide the fact that they have no idea what is wrong with the child.

'Abuse is abuse and ought to be called that. In all the cases I have been involved with I have not once been convinced that the parent in any way has abused the child or put the child in danger due to MSBP.

'But I have on the other hand at some occasions received evidence of medical malpractice and I see the accusations of MSBP as a way for medical staff to cover up their own mistakes. In many cases it appears that the family has to pay for bad doctorship and that is wrong. We cannot allow that to continue.'

To give credit where it is due, Americans were the first to get the Web sites defending parents accused of MSBP up, reflecting the beginnings of the Internet on that side of the Atlantic.

As mentioned in Chapter 4, Julie Patrick has set up what is regarded by many as the first stop on the Web for information – the MAMA site, Mothers Against Munchausen Allegations.

Opening with a quote from Exodus – 'You shall not bear false witness against your neighbour', the site reveals Julie's battles before going on to tell of what others have suffered throughout the years. It is one of the most comprehensive resources on the Internet – the only downside to it is that sometimes it is used as a reference tool by those trying to prove MSBP allegations.

On the opening page, Julie reveals the background to the site: 'M.A.M.A. was started in response to the fast-growing number of false allegations of MSBP. Increasingly, families across America, Britain, Australia, Canada and New Zealand are being destroyed by doctors and other professionals making unwarranted allegations against desperate mothers of chronically or critically ill children.

'The motives of the accusers can be multi-faceted. Often, allegations are used by a doctor or institution to evade a medical malpractice lawsuit, or to simply rid themselves of a troublesome mom when unable to diagnose a child's condition. MSBP experts are career building at the expense of children. Increasingly, this "diagnosis" is being deliberately misused by opposing parents in child custody suits. Many nurses and even doctors have been accused.

'The multiple stories we hear daily are ghastly.

'The word "syndrome" comes from the belief that the moms who supposedly "perpetrate" this type of abuse share common personality characteristics, motivated by their need for attention.

'In reality, the accusers, medical caregivers and Child Protective Service workers often perpetrate the real abuse. Never should a paediatrician engage in evaluating a parent's motive for the suspected abuse. A paediatrician must deal with science, not innuendo or personal bias.

'Even the most seasoned psychologists would avoid evaluating someone during a life crisis, yet this diagnosis relies on the unqualified evaluation of a parent's emotions during just such a time. It is serious misconduct to refer to a parent's demeanour as a basis for suspecting abuse.

'The madness continues as the "experts" debate this controversial diagnosis. Some say it is rare, while others claim it is common. The evolution of this diagnosis continues as even the name is debated... Factitious Disorder by Proxy, Meadow's Syndrome, Paediatric Falsification. While vying to be the top expert in this field, some claim it is a psychiatric condition, while others state it is a medical diagnosis, yet both approaches involve identifying the psychiatric motivation of the parent.

'Innocent mothers are profiled and removed from their needy child without any proof of wrongdoing. If the MSBP diagnosis is eventually proven to be erroneous and negligent, causing real harm or even death to the child, both the physician and CPS workers are covered under Good Faith Immunity Laws.

'The physician will proclaim that he had a legal responsibility to report even the slightest suspicion of abuse, even if he hadn't followed standard medical guidelines for researching all possible conditions which would produce the same symptoms. CPS, in turn, will cry that they were only responding to the expert opinion. Meanwhile the child is held as a medical hostage under the care of a physician or hospital who might do anything to protect their credibility.

'On the basis of a single phone call from a doctor, with no substantial evidence, CPS will rush in and confiscate a child without even interviewing the parents. Mom and dad will be instantly treated as criminals, guilty until proven innocent, and may lose the rest of their children as well. In the passion of the moment, the child will be held up in front of the mom like a carrot, causing her in desperation to agree to MSBP counselling or ridiculous psychiatric analysis or testing. Much of the purpose of this is to extract a false confession, while assuring the mother that co-operation will enable a quicker reunification. Financially and emotionally drained from their child's long illness, many moms are manipulated and entrapped because of their inability to fight. Once caught in the psychiatric state system, life becomes an indescribable nightmare for years.

'The MSBP agenda and the "child abuse industry" must be thoroughly exposed and the public must see who is really gaining from it. We must educate parents at risk that an MSBP diagnosis and profile can easily be fitted to include any mom who seriously advocates for her child.

'Laws must be changed rapidly to safeguard children and families. It is much too easy for a physician to make this accusation with no accountability if they are wrong. Hospitals, physicians and insurance companies have too much to gain by deterring a possible medical malpractice suit. If a child is taken for suspected abuse, at the very least, he or she should be immediately moved to an unbiased hospital for treatment with representatives of the parents enabled to advocate.

'Considering that a report by Harvard School of Public Health estimated 180,000 Americans die each year from medical mistakes, we should not be surprised at the surge of MSBP cases reported. This is a wealthy industry that does not want scrutiny and one that will take extraordinary measures to protect their image and income. That's why this "syndrome" was crafted broadly to imitate the actions of most advocating mothers – those who might "overutilise" the system.

'Thankfully, many media professionals are now seeing through the façade; academics and medical personnel are working to stop these atrocities!

'Large bureaucracies are crushing small defenceless families, yet many well-intentioned and influential government and media personnel are just starting to become aware of what is happening.

'We acknowledge that occurrences of child abuse are very real in our society and if a physician has real evidence to suspect child abuse, regardless of the motive of the perpetrator, it must be investigated and the perpetrators brought to swift and effective justice.

'In contrast, the agenda behind Munchausen Syndrome by

Proxy is often to be able to make an accusation without evidence, but by the Munchausen Syndrome by Proxy profile. The name of this "syndrome" evokes hysteria and it is the responsibility of the public and those that represent the public to question the motives of the accusing hospital and physician. If it is in fact abuse, call it by its real name and offer substantial proof.'

Another prominent American in the fight against MSBP is Barbara Bryan, Communications Director for the National Child Abuse Defense & Resource Center in Roanoke, Virginia.

She found herself involved with MSBP after being accused of it in the early 1980s (see Chapter 3) and has been a vocal opponent of it ever since. In her own words she is 'dedicated to exposing the flaws in Sir Roy Meadow's theory of mythical Munchausen Syndrome by Proxy'.

Barbara feels that in attacking MSBP accusations on a case-by-case basis people may be missing the wood for the trees and actually helping the condition to continue. She is now looking to change the situation by aiming at the source of the MSBP allegations – the work carried out by Meadow, Southall and others.

'For several years it seemed to me that a major mistake in MSBP defence, one I am working with attorneys to change, was and is that of fighting MSBP as a reality. It is a strategy that I believe simply entrenches it in the minds of judges and others as real, even though attorneys will point out that their client, the mother, does not have it.

'Worldwide, family justice advocates are at times getting nowhere with objective scientific evidence because courts and media could be mesmerised by the mystique of MSBP and we need disarming humour and an attitude of determination along the lines of reason and science to effect a shift in perspective.

'The courts are not proper crucibles for declaring science. So far, all the studies and reviews and commissions around the world officially undertaken to consider or reconsider MSBP have merely tightened its so-called definition, which is now exclusive and elastic to the point of impossibility of any successful defence.

'Certifying fraudulent New Clothesmakers for the Emperor with seemingly more rigid requirements – while nonetheless paying them both homage and tax monies – only adds insult and fantasy to obvious injury.

'As long as there are people who either find MSBP or find it does not exist in a certain mother and who "treat" it in any direction – beyond the inevitable post-traumatic stress disorders arising from maltreatment of one's ill child and innocent family by government agents and justice officials – MSBP will fail to die the ignoble death which the whole truth will ultimately inspire.

'I believe MSBP is an international urban legend along the lines of the Flat Earth Theory, a miserable holocaust of the home. I always write that we understand it is accepted in courts all around the world. So was the Flat Earth Theory and other aberrations of science in more unenlightened times.

'If you look at the original article it appears that MSBP has a single suspect basis which is Sir Roy's annoyed attitude at allegedly having been previously bested by a blood-switching mother who did not harm her child and who, Sir Roy agrees in the *Lancet* article, did not seek attention for herself, which is meant to be the whole point of MSBP.'

According to Barbara: 'Meadow admitted in private correspondence just before he retired that he had only ever submitted four research proposals to a local Research Ethics Committee in the whole of his working life as a doctor. Most of his published papers, even those that were published in the research sections of the journals, were the result of progressive advances in clinical practice for which no research consent was needed or obtained, or so he says.

'So how did someone with so little experience of formal research methods get to hold a professorship, get to be president of a royal college, get to be knighted? Why are his opinions on MSBP taken so seriously?

'And why do countries other than the UK allow themselves to be led by so-called experts from other countries? Why do they not conduct their own investigations into what has been said?

'Also, despite the claim that more than one child death in a family must be MSBP by a predictably murderous mother, any high school biology student, even in 1977, knew enough about DNA and inherited disorders to understand the increased likelihood of repeat problems or benefits for children of the same parents.

'If that is too difficult to grasp for the so-called experts, maybe we need to go back to school with Mendel who worked out a pretty simple ratio on inherited characteristics in the 19th century.'

Among other things, Barbara has called for openness of medical documentation and independent boards of review.

'When doctors order a drug or other treatment, including a vaccine cocktail for immature or weakened immune systems, which mistakenly injures a child, even in the hospital, how likely are they to volunteer that as the proximate "cause" of harm or death?

'It is vital to have all health records reviewed by truly independent and objective evaluators rather than accepting too many preferential presumptions for professionals and most others against parents and caretakers.'

Also in America, Pat Harris started up an e-mail list called Moms of the Heart 2. Unlike the other Web sites, this list is not just for mothers accused of MSBP. Instead it is a forum for experts and others not accused of MSBP who want to help others, to communicate with them and get more involved.

For Pat, the Internet has enabled her to tell others not to give in, to keep fighting.

'I was forced into MSBP as I was accused and lost three of my five children because of it. My cases were all dismissed and custody returned to me, though I do not have my children with me as my ex-husband has run off with them and gotten a court order from another state to be able to keep them.

'The message that I would like to send out to all that are being accused of MSBP is never give up, no matter what they say they can prove or whatever threats they may make. No matter what they get done in court, as long as your children are alive there is reason enough to fight. I have not seen or spoken to my two oldest children in three years, even though I have custody of them. Yet I keep fighting for them. I was accused a second time and that was overturned very quickly. The children returned in 22 hours.

'MSBP has to be and will be exposed for what it is and the Internet helps in that as it lets experts get in touch with others to offer their services to those who need it.'

Ruth Harville is also involved with both of the Moms of the Heart lists. Ruth was accused of MSBP and, just as she found it an aid in her darkest hours, she now helps others in their times of need.

'Julie Patrick and several others gave me the encouragement, lots of help and information to stay fighting. I really needed the guidance as to what in the hell I was fighting. I had no clue except I must be a really bad mother if they could just walk in with no evidence and take my little boy.

'My main goal out of all of this is for information to be available in one place for parents being accused of MSBP. After going through a case myself with no idea what it was or what was going to happen to my child or the rest of my family I felt that was one of the things needed most when our case was over.

'I spent 50 or 60 hours a week hunting for information to help our attorney. I never just thought something was not worth keeping – I saved it all. I knew within weeks of what started out as a nightmare what needed to be done to help parents and attorneys looking for information in my opinion.

'What there is now on the Web is lists of experts who are for and against MSBP, as well as as much information as can be found, scanned and typed in for parents not to have to waste valuable time looking for it. If you go to the Moms of the Heart list and look at the bookmark section, just wander through there. Many people are amazed at what has been compiled in one place.

'It takes a lot of time to make sure everything is still there. If it is not we hunt it back down and get it back up so the next time a parent needs it it is there. This is something we are doing right now with two people. It is going to take a while as there are thousands of links over there.

'My goal was for the information to be made open to the public as much as we could and still protect the parents on the list. Any new parent can give us a list of what their children's problems are and medications and we will help provide information for their attorney and them to help with fighting their case. We now have some mothers that have appeared in court as a support system and advocate for the parents. The attorneys for the parents know they can get everything we have and we will work on getting information for them. The system works but it is not easy. So many emotions are running wild when you lose your child.

'A place was needed where parents can get information but also the emotional support they need that was secure for them to ask questions without seeing it as "court, next round". They also need someplace that parents going through the same horrible ordeal can say, "Hey look, we have all been there, stop letting them kick you down and fight for your children". This is easier taken then by someone who has lost their children. It takes motivation to get the parents moving and stay moving at times. Fear, their hope failing and mostly missing their children makes it hard sometimes to keep fighting when you keep losing at each round. But you do lose and lose forever if you stop. In my opinion if there is another day then you have hope. I would never have stopped fighting for my son and I encourage parents to do the same. If we give up, the accusers win.

'I know how lost I felt when my son was snatched out of my arms in the doctor's office and I was given a court order. My life almost stopped right there.

'I also knew if I stopped to feel sorry or have shock my son would not survive. [Parents] need a place to go and vent, cry and have someone there that is not going to attack them, just support them and continue to help them in their fight to get their children back.

'I have met or spoken to about 200 or more parents. This is not a rare thing that is being done to harm our children, it is something that needs to be stopped and it won't be until somehow the truth is exposed to the public in a way they see that, "Hey, this can and will happen to my daughter, mother, sister, wife or even myself if we don't put a stop to it". The first step in making it stop is getting some of these cases into the federal court houses with newspapers, TV, whatever there to make sure the public knows what is going on.

'I want them to see what the places we take our children to be healed are doing to harm them and yes, sometimes even kill them, all for money, to protect themselves from malpractice and research. I want doctors and state officials to start having to be responsible again. There is no family that would sue a doctor if he said, "You know, we don't have a clue what is going on with your child or at least what is causing it. But we will help all we can and also help to find someone else that just might have the answer we don't". Our children are being affected by so many things today that children just 50 years ago never had to worry about. Air pollution, toxic waste and so on.

'There are more medically fragile children than ever. Asthma is at an all-time high in children and climbing. Cancer, as well as so many of the medical problems that we did not worry about children having, are now affecting the lives of our children.

'Children are receiving medications that have not been tested to be safe, thus causing more damage. Autism is another disorder that has grown at a rate that is unbelievable, with no answers as to why. If they want to use their money from grants and such, use it to find a cure for our children, not accuse us of causing it. We as parents, be it natural or adopted, do not want and will not sit there and watch our child die just because they feel our child is not important enough for medical care but just a research guinea pig.

'My hope and prayer has been since day one that my child or no one else's ever has to spend one second away from their parents because of MBSP. When it is gone and when it is not harming children any more then I will be at peace for what happened to my child, my family and myself – not until then.

'Different moms react differently after being on the list and then their cases end. Some, when their cases are over, go back to try to have a life again but many stay to offer support and help to the next family. When MSBP is over we plan to make it a cooking club or something – anything but a place where so much pain has passed through.'

Tamie Dell is another high profile campaigner on the Internet. She has also been accused of MSBP. She had lawyers who helped her through her case but even after she was cleared and the case closed, she still felt it hang over her.

'After I was exonerated and the children were home, I found myself still living under a cloud of suspicion. Not only had I lost most, if not all, of my friends, as they felt I must have done "something" to have been accused, I was also living with an abusive husband who was looking at the experience as a way to cash in for himself.

'As legal action was pursued against the state, I would be followed by the police officer that had me arrested and one CPS worker whenever I went out. All of this time I knew no one that had been through this, nor did I realise that there really were others out there that I could talk to.

'I wound up deciding that it didn't matter that I was found to be innocent and the state's attorney general had ordered my case closed – they were determined to get my children. Since I believed this and had no support I tried suicide. Although I am not proud of this, it did however finally get me some help.

'The psychiatrist that I had in the hospital continued to treat me and helped me to get therapy to deal with what I had been through. For the next two years and a few months these people were the only support that I had. They were also the only ones other than my immediate family that believed that I had done nothing to my children, other than strongly advocate for their well being.

'Since I felt so alone through all of this, I had a very hard time coping with everything that I had been through and eventually came to believe that there must be something wrong with me.

'Obviously, I did have a problem coping with everything, but felt that it was much more than the inability to cope with what had been a situation that was out of my control and abusive to myself and my children on the part of the state. I lived with my own fears that this could and would happen again. I also lived with three children that had nightmares and a huge fear of people that children commonly look at as their protectors – police, doctors and so on.

'In the late summer of 1999 I was given a computer by a friend. This same friend got me hooked up to the Internet. Before this time I had never touched a computer. I would play with it, slowly teaching myself how to type and also how to use the Internet.

'During this time I had also started writing about my experiences, as was suggested by my therapist. Since I was writing about what I had been through I thought it would be a good idea to see what I could find out on the Internet about MSBP. This led me to the MAMA site.

'Needless to say I was floored to discover that there were others out there that had been through this. For some reason that I can't remember I e-mailed the list and simply said that I had been through this accusation too. I don't think that I even put my name on the e-mail as I didn't e-mail it from my regular e-mail.

'About a week later I was phoned by someone in Texas asking if I had gotten my children back and wanting to put me on a support list for moms that had been accused. At that point I was still being very cautious. I didn't say much to the group at first but more just read the stories of what was going on. I was overwhelmed by what I was seeing. I had at one point said something about who the expert for the state was in my case and that we had gotten her discredited.

'Julie Patrick contacted me in October of 1999 concerning a mother that was facing these charges. They needed someone that could help them to discredit the state's expert. I had no idea what I could do but agreed to talk to this mother and her attorney. When I spoke to this mother I could hear the desperation in her voice and the fear for her children. Obviously I knew all too well how she felt. I also knew what it was like to go through this alone. I agreed to talk to her attorney. When we spoke I gave him information on how to reach my attorney and also gave my attorney permission to tell him anything about my case that would help this family and her attorney. The case was dismissed and the family reunited. I was told how my part in everything helped. I then realised that I could help, even if only in a very small way. That, with also knowing the pain and isolation that someone feels that goes through this, is why I do it. I wouldn't wish what I went through on any mother. I also can't bear the thought of any child going through what my children went through.

'I realise that being accused of this and having your children removed from your home is probably the most horrible thing that any accused parent has ever been through. I can see how this can easily make someone want to give up. I also realise that many mothers want to have someone come in and take care of everything for them. As horrible as things are for the accused parent, things are probably worse for your children.

'The only person that truly cares what your children are going through is you. Therefore, since they are totally helpless in this instance it is time for you to stand up and fight. If you want to wait for the proverbial knight in shining armour to come along and fix everything for you, you might as well sign the papers for the government to have your children. Although there may be people there that care and will help, if you as the accused parent do not help yourself and your children, they won't come home.

'I realise that this may be harsh. However, every child that I know who has come home, Mom played a big role in getting them home. This may not be the outcome in all cases. However, when the parents do not fight and fight hard for their children the children are lost.

'In my case I worked very hard to help my attorneys. I asked questions. I pushed the limits. I stepped on toes. I spoke out and did so loudly, against the advice of my attorneys. I didn't have anything to hide as I didn't do anything. I gathered information against those working for the state. I let them know I had it and that I intended to use it. I let them know that no one would be able to shut me up. I made copies of the evidence that I had and distributed it so that the authorities couldn't find it. I went into law libraries and looked up the laws myself. I held everyone involved accountable for their actions. I pointed out that they were the criminals, siting what laws it was that they were breaking. I let it be known that I intended for this all to eventually be public.

'I also let them know that I wouldn't stop until my children were home and safe.'

Nine

Maria, Scotland

Scotland. A country inspired by freedom fighters and those who took up arms against those who would try to take away what was rightfully theirs. Now things are a little different but whereas before a man had a chance to stand and fight for his family, nowadays lawyers can make that almost impossible, as the Kents discovered when they were accused of MSBP.

The Kents had moved to Scotland in 1990, settling in the central belt and finding themselves within easy travelling distance of the main cities of Glasgow and Edinburgh. John Kent had brought his family here for a few reasons. The main one was that he had been offered a well-paying job on the oil rigs of the north-east coast near Aberdeen. The central belt was close enough for him to travel home once a fortnight. Second, it would give his brother, Grant, who lived with him and John's wife Maria, a chance to get over the loss of his wife in a car crash. Financially he was fine, but mentally was another story and John had insisted that he move north with the couple.

There were no children involved, as their teenage daughter Joan had stayed behind in England to study, but Maria and John had let it be known that they would be interested in being foster parents. They did not want to adopt full-time, but had no problems being temporary fosters.

Eventually they were accepted into the foster parent scheme. Grant was very much seen as acting as a father figure for the two weeks every month that John was offshore.

Over the years the three became outstanding foster parents and were praised for the love, warmth and wonderful care they gave the children that passed through their doors. Many of the children stayed in touch long after they had moved on.

In 1995 they had two children staying with them when a third came along, Karen, aged 10.

Karen was a quiet girl but when it was revealed that she came from a poor background with a history of abuse and alcoholic parents, this was understood. Slowly she came out of her shell. She never seemed like the most enthusiastic of children, but again this was put down to her background.

They liked and loved the girl though and they even considered the possibility of seeing if they could adopt her or be made her legal guardians, as there was something about her that touched their hearts.

Then in the winter of 1995 she came down with a really bad case of pneumonia, from which she slowly recovered. After it though, she never seemed the same, more distant than before, as well as even more lethargic – too lethargic for even doctors to put it down to a combination of her previous life and hormonal changes at that age.

On a daily basis she started to complain of headaches, muscle aches, nausea, sore throat and difficulty sleeping, walking and thinking. She was also showing sensitivity to light and sound and over time the headaches got worse.

The family had never had a really ill child before. There had been the odd broken bone here and there, but nothing out of the ordinary. Maria took Karen's illness worse than the men. She had come from a similar background and so wanted this girl to have all the chances in life that Maria felt she deserved.

They suggested to the doctor that perhaps Karen was suffering from a form of ME, the so-called 'Yuppie flu', which would match the symptoms being presented. The elderly doctor dismissed their claims and told them that she was probably suffering from having been given too much attention when she was ill and was now playing it up to keep getting that level of attention, as he could find nothing wrong with her.

This continued for weeks, with Karen eventually being referred to specialists. Unfortunately, due to successive underfunding by governments, the UK's National Health Service does not have the money for specialists to see people right away. Very often people can wait more than six months for an appointment. Karen was no different and during that time she took more and more painkillers to try to numb the pain.

Meanwhile the Kents found themselves under investigation by the local council for keeping Karen away from school. They were told that they could not keep her off indefinitely without medical reasons and their doctor had already said on repeated occasions that there was nothing wrong with her.

At one of the last meetings with the doctor, they were introduced to his replacement, a younger, more caring-looking doctor. However, he agreed with his elder colleague and suggested that Karen needed nothing more than 'a good kick up the backside' to get her going again.

The new doctor also asked the parents if they thought at all – even the smallest hint – that she was faking it or perhaps that it was all psychological and she might be suffering from Munchausen Syndrome to get attention.

The Kents said they did not think so. If she was faking, they said, she deserved an Oscar for managing it for months, 24 hours a day.

The specialists also said that they could find nothing wrong with Karen, but conceded that she might be suffering from depression. She was given a number of treatments to try to lift her, but all these succeeded in doing was making her sick, which did not help her weight, already dangerously low due to her lack of eating.

It was around this time, just before the start of the new school year, that the council started taking more of an interest in the Kents. The Kents believed it was just routine foster parent check-ups, interviewing the adults and the children, inspecting the home and so on. Therefore they were not surprised when they never heard anything back in terms of a report from the visit. They assumed they had been given the foster parent equivalent of a clean bill of health.

That winter, Karen came down with another attack of pneumonia. Her little impoverished frame was in no state to withstand the assault and she was hospitalised. While she was there, the Kents were asked if the social work department of the local council and their doctor could visit them at home.

Puzzled, the Kents said yes. When the day came it became clear that it was anything but a social visit, with the doctor and three social workers all looking as if they had just come from a funeral.

They explained that the doctor suspected the family of Munchausen Syndrome by Proxy. After explaining what it was, they told the Kents that Grant and Maria were the ones being accused of it. They were also accused of acting independently. The professionals' reasoning was simplistic. Maria was doing it to get attention as she resented John going away for at least two weeks every month, while Grant was looking for attention to help him resolve the death of his wife.

Grant did not take this well, leaping across the table and getting into a tumbling fight with the nearest social worker, raining blows on his head. He was eventually pulled off and he stormed out but the Kents knew it would not help matters.

What had added to it was that when the doctor had commented that she looked tired, Karen had said it was because the Kents kept waking her up early after nights where she would get no sleep. She also pointed out that she found the food in their house to be very salty.

Karen had also told the doctor that they made her take the medicine that she had thrown up. This was correct. They made her take the same type of medicine and vitamin tablets that she had thrown up, but not the actual pills and capsules that she had vomited. The distinction did not become clear until afterwards. The doctor had just taken the expression as it sounded.

The social workers also informed the Kents that other children had complained of being woken up early in the morning and not always getting treatment for injuries, being left to walk with sprained ankles and so on.

Both John and Grant admitted to this, saying that it normally happened when the children were playing sports. They had felt that it was good for the children – if they were capable – to be self-reliant and try to get over the pain if they could. For bad injuries they had of course not left the children to walk home.

It would later be revealed that Karen's complaints of early rises were because that was the only time the Kents could get her emergency medical appointments, so she had to be up first thing. The lack of sleep came from her being in pain in the first place, which necessitated the medical emergencies.

The salty-tasting food was, years later, put down to the fact that the adults all had poor tastebuds and had not considered the children in this as the adults thought they had normal tastebuds. The children had never complained to them, being far too polite or liking the salty taste, so the adults never knew anything was amiss.

The children's complaints about early morning awakenings were also correct. It was a large house, but there was only one bathroom and the children had to be up in good time to be clean before going to school. To the children though, any time in the morning was early morning.

The social workers had learned all of this while investigating possible MSBP. As they were already looking at that area, any claims of cruelty gave them more 'proof'. They had gone in with their solution and in their blinkered view the facts seemed to fit the theory.

As she recovered from the pneumonia the doctors started to suspect that Karen had an eating disorder and should be treated by a psychiatrist. Karen had been unable to eat for a month. Her weight loss became critical. When the doctors decided on tube feeding, her improved nutrition helped her nausea, she began to eat and she grew stronger and more animated. Her headaches remained severe but she had more energy. The Kents began to hope that she would soon be able to return home.

While Karen remained in hospital the other two children were still with them, but life was being made awkward for them at school, as it had become common knowledge that the Kents were being investigated for child abuse. With word getting out that they were being looked at as bad foster parents, possibly worse, a number of things happened. The two children were shunned by their friends at school as parents warned their own children to stay away.

The Kents also had to change their phone number due to the number of abusive calls they were getting at all hours of the day and night, something that was not helping the two children get any sleep.

Rocks and various objects were constantly being thrown at the Kents' car, except when they had the children in it. When they were in it, the worst that happened was spitting and shouting, something that also happened to the Kents very occasionally when they were out in public.

Once the council became aware of this, the children were removed from the Kents' home and the Kents were informed that until the allegations were cleared up, they would not be receiving any more children to look after.

The Kents requested a different psychiatrist to examine Karen and review her records. He found no indicators of abuse or an eating disorder. This, plus weight gain, secured Karen's discharge, but within a month she was back in hospital as she had suffered a relapse.

A new doctor at the hospital did not help with their attempts at encouraging Karen to get better, saying that if she helped them to help her, things would improve a lot. What the Kents were unaware of at that time was that she was also being promised that she could spend more time with them if she improved.

She was released after some weight gain, but then came the final insult.

The Kents were told that Karen was to be taken away from them and they were to be charged with causing her serious harm.

From that point on, everything the Kents heard about Karen, they heard through their lawyer.

Doctors were ordering Karen to see them each week, be weighed at the hospital, keep a log of everything she ate and have random drug screens. She could have no medications of any kind. She had to return to school full time immediately.

She and the Kents were also to submit to psychological evaluations and individual and family counselling at the Kents' expense.

After the case ended, the Kents learnt that during this period Karen got worse. She was placed with new foster parents under the constant fear that she would be taken from them. For days she cried and for months she had terrible nightmares. She had nothing to relieve her pain. She was in bed except for the time she was in school and for the weekly hospital trip. Because of headaches, nausea and fatigue she often had to leave class to go to the nurse's office.

After two months, and just before the start of the Kents' trial, a doctor diagnosed that Karen had classic depression, which had led to episodes of anorexia and bulimia.

Meanwhile the psychologist who performed the ordered evaluation had found no pathology in any of the Kents and said that MSBP was not a correct diagnosis. He recommended that Karen's symptoms be relieved by the use of medication, that home schooling be provided, and that the Kents have counselling to help them deal with the crises they had experienced.

Nevertheless, the trial went ahead. Karen was too ill to give testimony in person and instead a statement was read out. She said in it that she had enjoyed her time with the Kents and would have liked to have been adopted by them. She did not think they had ever tried to harm her, just look after her as best they could.

The two-week-long trial saw a lot of medical jargon thrown about that confused many of the people involved. Maria was accused of doing everything for attention, even becoming a foster parent. She denied all of this, including the MSBP accusations, pointing out that she could not win because if she denied it, she looked as if she was covering up because after all, who would admit to it, while if she admitted it, she then appeared guilty.

At the end of the trial, it was felt that there was not enough evidence to convict Maria of anything. Grant was fined for his assault of the social worker, but that was the end of the legal matter.

To this day, very few people seem to know what was wrong with Karen. The Kents have heard that she still shows the same symptoms as she did before, which they feel backs up their argument that there was some form of ME involved. They will never know as they are forbidden to have any contact with the child they almost called their own.

After the trial, the family moved back to England. The promise that life in Scotland had offered had been destroyed by the actions of the council and the medical staff. Using the Internet, they have kept their eye out for the people and hospitals involved in their case and they have come to the conclusion that while those involved may have been acting with the best of intentions, when you are dealing with something that may have repercussions for the rest of someone's life, best intentions are not enough by far.

The Kents hope that one day, when Karen is over 18, she will be able to get in touch with them and they can talk about her past. While they cannot prosecute, they do hope that they will be able to go public with all the names and details of what happened to them, in the hope that others will not be hurt in the way they were.

Ten

Neither For Nor Against

Not everyone is for or against MSBP. There are those who either sit on the fence or have come into the subject without being an accused sufferer or having a paediatric-based medical background. Some of them have come away believing that MSBP is very real, others quite the opposite. Some are still unsure if there is such a condition.

In Glasgow, Dr Robert McWilliam has summed up the problem for both sides succinctly, saying: 'If you are wrong it may be hurtful for the parent, but if you're right and you don't write it down it could be potentially lethal for a child.

'If I suspected a mother had this, I would discuss it with colleagues rather than jumping to conclusions. But there is no harm in putting down a suspected diagnosis in case notes and not a confirmed diagnosis.'

In America, Tom Ryan is one attorney who, after learning of MSBP, is starting to fight for the rights of accused women. Of course he is only allowed to take one side in any matter, that of his client, but he has dealt with enough MSBP cases to have formed a strong opinion in only a few short years.

He said: 'To me this is reminiscent of the fairytale *The Emperor's New Clothes.*

'I have consulted with the most pre-eminent medical scholars in the fields of genetics, microbiology, immunology, neurology, psychiatry and many other areas to find that the allegations against the mothers were as nonexistent as the Emperor's clothing.

'The essence of MSBP, as described by the so-called experts, seems to be that the mother medically maltreats her child to gain the attention or approval of doctors. The reasons given by these experts as to why a mother would do this smack of misogyny, or as I like to call it in court, pure, unadulterated, "mommy bashing".

'The reasons testified to range from "women are much more manipulative than men" to "women have become enamoured with doctors as saviours, through the medium of daytime and night-time medical soap dramas".

'But one of the problems, to me anyway, is that the experts cannot agree on what to call MSBP, much less agree on how to define it. In a short period of time it has been given a handful of names including "Munchausen Syndrome by Proxy", "Munchausen by Proxy Syndrome", "Munchausen by Proxy" and "Factitious Disorder by Proxy".

'Each of these labels carries with it a vastly different definition, each more vague and equivocal than the next. Is this a mental health disorder residing within the mother?'

There are many important questions left begging. Unfortunately, the relevant medical community cannot agree on what the answers to these questions are.

'And then there is the so-called profile used in identification,' continues Ryan. 'One point in this is that if the mother is convincing in her denial of the allegations, then that goes against her and can be a sign of MSBP. But how can it be?

'One can easily imagine an innocent mother testifying sincerely and convincingly about her innocence, only to have the judge check off one more element of the profile as having been met. Of course, if she is nervous about testifying in court and appears less than convincing, that will be counted against her as well.'

It is a lose–lose scenario.

'But court complexity and cases do not help as the literature on MSBP is replete with warnings that only those doctors and scientists who are well versed in the supposed permutations of this "disorder" can see. This can have the side effect that by the time an MSBP case gets to the judge, it is replete with dubious experts, social workers, detectives and nervous treating physicians who by now have all jumped on the Munchausen bandwagon.

'Court is also a problem in terms of finance because the average mother has no chance of winning her case and keeping her family together because of the expense involved in going up against the large resources of a state.'

One of the most acclaimed books in recent years on the subject of MSBP has been *Disordered Mother or Disordered Diagnosis?* by David Allison and Mark Roberts, who both teach philosophy at the State University of New York at Stony Brook and are also experts in psychoanalysis.

It is an excellent read, though very dry in places, but the message the authors present cannot be denied. By the final chapter you are left in no doubt that despite the widespread conviction among legal and psychiatric experts that MSBP actually exists, the evidence sustaining it is insubstantial and logically flawed.

The book also draws very close parallels with the Salem witch-hunts of the 17th century, looking at the sort of hysteria that gripped so-called experts then and now.

The authors show, in painstaking detail at times, how psychiatric descriptions and literature on MSBP has been thoroughly circular and self-justifying. They also point out their belief that MSBP's 'father', Munchausen Syndrome, has served as a catchphrase for chronically and disagreeably ill patients who share nothing beyond an ability to confuse and eventually antagonise their physicians.

They come to the conclusion that if the diagnosis is real it has serious social implications, as families lose their children, who are placed into care or fostered.

Helen Hayward-Brown, tutor at the Department of Public Health of Charles Sturt University in Bathurst, Australia, carried out a study into MSBP for her Ph.D. In her findings she remembers it being a difficult experience as she interviewed more than 25 families to find out their experiences.

'At the outset of my investigations I knew that I would uncover some unpleasant experiences, but nothing prepared me for the sinister turn my work would take. To make matters worse the sinister turn was generally the hospital environment.

'By this I mean the extreme reaction on the part of some medical professionals when they could not find out what was wrong with a child and the mother was being labelled with MSBP. I found increasing numbers of this as the years went on through historical research.'

Hayward-Brown found a number of patterns in her work, including that once a mother is merely suspected of MSBP she is treated as if guilty. The old saying in the UK about innocent until proven guilty did not seem to apply here and this was just one of many areas in which the conduct of paediatricians and psychiatrists is highly questionable.

What she also found was that diagnoses and accusations were being made by very senior specialists in the hospital environment, who may have had little firsthand knowledge of the families involved. What worried her even more was that these diagnoses were sometimes being made after only one consultation and even by post or e-mail at times. In her own words: 'For me, the deceit and betrayal of the medical profession was almost incomprehensible.'

Hayward-Brown's research also suggests that those accused of MSBP may actually be nothing more than pawns in the medical battlefield, as different specialities try to exercise more power and influence.

To back this up, she points to paediatricians like Roy Meadow saying that psychiatrists should be excluded from diagnosis, while psychiatrists such as Herbert Schreir feel GPs and paediatricians with long-term family contact should be excluded, as they can be perceived to be in collusion with the mother.

Hayward-Brown also points out that most of the literature produced on the subject is found in paediatric journals and notes that 'as a result, diagnosis of this serious mental illness is being made by medical practitioners with no psychiatric background'.

Writing in a 1995 edition of the *Archives of Disease in Childhood*, Dr C. J. Morley highlighted a number of practical concerns about

MSBP that have to be addressed by everyone in the field. She used the paper to express what she called her concerns about MSBP, particularly the name of it and the baggage that it brought with it.

She noted the problems both sides face, saying 'It is important to protect a child who is being harmed by his mother. It is equally important not to harm the child by falsely accusing his mother of Munchausen Syndrome by Proxy, thereby breaking up the family'.

She noted that after Beverley Allitt's trial, MSBP was a loaded phrase, charged with the emotion of her crimes, and anyone accused of it afterwards, whether innocent or guilty, was associated with all that Allitt had done (despite the fact that she did not have MSBP, according to psychiatric reports. The phrase stuck from the trial).

Morley feels that a better way of identifying what has happened would be to state the injury – poisoning, starvation, suffocation, tampering with medicines or medical examination and so on – as MSBP ultimately does not say what has happened to the affected person.

Morley agrees that the MSBP criteria are vague and can be misinterpreted. For example, with regard to children who are taken to their doctors on a regular basis, it may be that the child is genuinely ill a lot or that the parent is very anxious about their child's health and takes them to the doctor for any cough or bump.

As for parents coming across as emotional and frustrated, Morley explains this as the natural concern a parent can have, along with being upset by the doctor not listening fully.

Denial of causing the child harm is, for Morley, one that can be easily explained – the child is genuinely ill. What worries Morley though is the allegations of blackmail. She has heard that mothers are told they have to confess to harming their child before they can have treatment and if they do not confess they are unlikely to get their children back.

Morley was also able to shed light on the mysterious matter of illnesses clearing up after children have been taken into care.

She points out two reasons for this. First, many childhood illnesses like apnoea or vomiting get better with time and second, the timing could be such that the conditions clear up just as the children are taken into care.

Her report also carried an examination of the other areas medical experts look at.

With regard to inconsistent medical histories and doctors not recognising symptoms, that is something that will differ from doctor to doctor, depending on experience. One doctor may not recognise an illness and think 'MSBP', while another doctor may know exactly what it is. Morley also points out that doctors should know that not every treatment will work or may trigger adverse reactions.

As for the parents having excellent knowledge, this would not be uncommon with parents who have ill children as they may have researched the matter out of concern, not malice. Ditto for parents who seem to fit in at hospitals – this may be because they are there on a regular basis and know their way about and the staff.

Mothers always being present at illnesses is, according to Morley, also easily explained by the fact that concerned mothers are more often than not the parent that spends more time with the child.

One area Morley urges extreme caution in is histories and backgrounds. An instance of this is the way the mother tells details. As her report notes, 'Some mothers are poor at giving a detailed account of a life-threatening event. Rarely are they told to give a scientifically accurate report to the doctors'.

As for the mothers and their own history, especially with allegations of abuse, Morley notes that this is an area that needs careful history note-taking, scrutiny of the notes and possibly even confidential discussion with the mothers' doctors.

'It is primarily a medical diagnosis and must be based on sound medical practice. This means taking a very careful history, eliciting exact details about what has happened. It may mean talking to the mother for hours to get a clear understanding about all the episodes, why she is concerned, and her own background.'

Morley has fears though that the medical experts may not always take the necessary time with patients. She cites as an example a recent case where the mother briefly saw the consultant during her children's illnesses but who did not take time to sit down and talk to her until he came with a social worker to say she was accused of Munchausen Syndrome by Proxy.

In concluding her report she says that MSBP is a term which should no longer be used as it does not give an accurate description of the illness and the phrase itself is emotionally loaded.

However, Morley's article did not go unchallenged. Dr A. D. Milner of the Department of Paediatrics at the United Medical and Dental School, St Thomas's Hospital, London, believes that MSBP does exist and has to be confronted.

Talking about the actual label MSBP he said that he remained convinced MSBP is a useful term that has not been invalidated by its misuse on a single occasion, which in his opinion was the Beverley Allitt trial.

Dr Milner points out that having numerous criteria does raise the chances that the child is at risk if the criteria are met.

Milner does admit that at times paediatricians do not always manage to listen carefully to the information provided to them. He also disagrees with Morley's belief that inconsistent histories are not much use, saying, 'Much weight has been placed on the importance of identifying inconsistencies in the description of events in the diagnosis of child abuse.

'If they are helpful in that condition they are also useful in the identification of Munchausen Syndrome by Proxy.'

So who is right and who is wrong? The truth is that no one can tell and people have to form their own opinion. Having an opinion is not dangerous, but not keeping an open mind on the matter when a case presents itself could be very dangerous for all concerned.

Eleven

Tammie, USA

For most people, having a child is a natural thing, yet it is one of the saddest facts of life that all too often the people who want children the most cannot have them and the more they try, the more they despair. This was the problem for Tammie and her husband John. They had been trying for years for a child but Tammie had fallen pregnant on a number of occasions only to miscarry at various stages in term.

The couple were despairing of ever having children, when an old high school friend got in touch, saying that he and his wife were about to have a fourth baby, and it was a baby too many as they had no means of supporting it, so would Tammie like to adopt?

According to Tammie it was not an option the family had ever considered, but there they were – someone who knew Tammie had asked her if she would look after his child because he thought she could be a good mother.

This was no hit and miss adoption. The biological parents would know their child was going to a good home, while Tammie and John would finally have their dream come true and be parents.

Sadly, the old adage of be careful what you wish for because you might just get it was to come all too true for the couple.

But the sad days were far away from everyone's mind in 1989 as Tammie and John met the mother to make sure she was certain it was what she wanted.

Tammie still remembers the first meeting well.

'We had decided that if the mother was absolutely positive that adoption was what she wanted then we would go ahead with it.

'I met my son's birth mother as she was starting her seventh month of pregnancy. She had had no prenatal care except for the one appointment at the beginning of her fourth month to confirm the pregnancy.

'She told me that she had been binge drinking during her first trimester, but quit when she found out about the pregnancy. She also smoked a pack or so a day of cigarettes, and the birth father told me they smoked pot during her last month or so.'

However, everything seemed to be going well for a birth just a few days before Christmas 1989, but little Matthew came into the world two weeks early on 7 December at 3.12 am. He weighed 5 lb 5 oz and Tammie remembers it being a noisy birth, with her soon-to-be son screaming, sounding outraged and making noises like an angry kitten. His health was fine apart from having to spend a few days under some special lights to treat jaundice and he was home with his adopted parents in time for Christmas.

From the beginning though, Tammie started to notice some strange things about her son and while she dismissed some of this as a mother being overprotective, she still had nagging doubts.

'While he was a great little baby, there were some odd things about him. You couldn't hold him to feed him at first so he had to be propped to be fed. He also never wanted to lie down in someone's arms, but always be held upright.

'However, like all babies he was a noisy one and I don't think there's one single photograph of him from his first week or so where he's not screaming.

'He seemed to really bond well with us and according to the babysitter we had, he cried all the time when I or my husband was not around.

'Over the coming weeks and months he developed as a child should, growing not only as a baby, but also into our hearts. He first rolled over at only a few weeks old and I thought he was an amazing little guy, he was my pride and joy.

'He soon settled down and became a healthy, happy, bubbly baby. His only problem was on a couple of occasions his body went stiff and his eyes rolled back when his temperature went over 103°, but I was told this was not abnormal and that he would outgrow it, which he did.

'He grew quickly and as he started hitting his milestones I noticed they were a little off.

'For example, he said "mama" at three months, walked at around 16 months and got his eyeteeth first, but knowing that children mature at their own rate, I didn't fret too much about this.'

The first two years, while not perfect, were typical for new parents, with every bump, fall and cut being fussed over, relatives visiting and making funny noises to entertain the child, nappy changes in the middle of the night, baby throwing up over new clothes, worries about bathwater temperature even after dipping elbows in to check it – the usual family matters that can be looked back at and laughed about in later years.

But it was in 1992 that Tammie's concerns about Matthew's health started to grow noticeable. To everyone.

'He would cry until he turned blue and passed out, he had no anxiety about strangers, which was really unusual, and was a serious climber, with the top of the refrigerator quickly becoming one of his favourite spots.

'That was bad enough but he was also turning into a regular Houdini, vanishing if you took your eye off him for even a second, able to open doors that he should never have been able to and when you know your child likes to climb, you really do panic about where he's gone and you only hope you can find him before you hear the noise of something breaking or him falling.

'He was also becoming very aggressive, with one of his favourite games being to headbutt mom really hard, and was spouting off foul language.

'Of course other mothers and families starting offering me all the usual motherly advice over what to do with a challenging child, some of which was contradictory – spank him, ignore him, take a break – but regardless of what I tried he just got more and more extreme.'

That year also saw the family break up and divorce, with Tammie receiving custody of Matthew although his adopted father was welcome to see him at any time, though he rarely did. Tammie has never put this down to any deliberate maliciousness, poor parenting or bitterness on the part of John. They both knew that after the split he had his own problems to sort out.

After getting over the split, mother and son were both hospitalised for different illnesses. Matthew spent six days in hospital for lymphadenitis, while Tammie ended up with double pneumonia and was in hospital for a week.

After they were released from hospital, it was decided that the best thing for all concerned was a move to her parents' home in Big Timber, Montana. The idea had been thought up by Tammie's mother, who thought it would allow the pair to heal, physically as well as emotionally, and become healthy again.

They stayed there for about a year, building up their strength and confidence in dealing with the world, during which time Matthew and Tammie's dad became very close. The two of them seemed good for each other, with the dad calming down the youngster and the father picking up some of the toddler's energy and vitality.

After a year in Big Timber, Tammie decided it was time to move on with life and get back to college, so they moved away, but no sooner had the two of them got settled in Laurel when Tammie's father came down unexpectedly with cancer and died fairly quickly, which was a horrible blow to all concerned. While Tammie had to deal with her own sadness, as well as that of her mother, she had even more worries with Matthew.

'My little man, now four, worried me, as he asked a lot of questions but he never cried or showed sadness about it. However, emotionally it must have been affecting him because he did begin to change as he started suffering violent rages, which were far more than temper tantrums and were closer to an adult's rage than that of a child.

'It terrified me, both because of what was happening and

because of the helplessness I was feeling, as I didn't know what to do – I was calling my mother in tears. I ended up taking him to a counsellor, thinking maybe he could work through some sort of grief counselling or therapy with him.

'Instead, he ran a bunch of developmental tests and told me there was nothing wrong with my child, except that I needed to be more strict with him.

'So I started to be more strict with him but nothing changed, except that saying "no" would set him off in a fit, resolving nothing.'

A vow made to her father before he died meant that Tammie had to put away the life that she had set up for herself in Laurel and return to nearer Big Timber to look after her mother.

'I had promised my father that I would look after my mother and ensure that she was safe, so I found myself moving again, this time to Livingston.

'Once there we started to go through a number of babysitters as my son became more and more off kilter. Years later one sitter told me that he had spoken to her about the "voices" he heard telling him to stab his mommy and run away.

'She never told me at the time because she thought he was seeking attention and his behaviour was all down to bad parenting.

'As his self-esteem seemed to plummet, his rage went up. I had to pay a portion of the repair bill for windows that he and three of his little buddies broke. Meanwhile, some other kids in the neighbourhood refused to play with him because he was so aggressive.'

But Tammie was managing to cope and was getting her own life back on a steady course, while looking after Matthew. Things were looking up for a while when Tammie was accepted into university. She hoped this was the beginning of better days, but her hopes were to be in vain. The good days were merely the calm before the storm.

'We had moved again so that we could be nearer the university campus and it was here that his behaviour came to a head. It was about a month after we moved when he had an eight-hour rage with alternating periods of bizarre behaviour and sobbing bouts where he'd just cling to me.

'I took him to the paediatrician's office where he noted this behaviour in the record. He gave me prescriptions and sent us home, but the medication didn't work and my son kept fitting.

'I was exhausted and scared to death with no one to turn to – what was wrong with my baby? I ended up calling 911 to ask the local police officers for an escort to the ER with him as I couldn't hold him like this and drive.

'They refused to take us in a squad car and instead called an ambulance. We were taken to the ER, where they finally gave him more medication to get him calmed down and while that solved the next few hours, I knew it was not the end of the troubles as I feared what would happen when the medication ran out and there was no one about to help me.

'I knew this was not something that was going to be cured by a few days in bed, chicken soup and a course of antibiotics.'

Matthew's paediatrician embarked on a full attempt to try to help the family, referring them to a neurologist and a psychiatrist, after which it was decided to refer Matthew to a day treatment centre.

This started in December 1996. The focus from the start was that Matthew could control his fits, as they felt they were due to depression as well as conflict between the child and parent. Things improved for a while with Matthew stabilising, though he was, according to Tammie, 'by no means cured'.

He was discharged nine months later, with Tammie then getting help from AWARE, a youth case management group for mentally ill children. They assist with hospitalisation as needed, arrange for respite care and get mentors for the children, and they were a good help, giving the exhausted mother some relaxation time to recuperate. But all her spare time was soon to be taken up fighting accusations of bad parenting.

'Not long after Matthew was discharged from day care, a Department of Family Services worker came to my home, spoke and chatted away with me for a while and then told me that I had been accused of a syndrome called Munchausen by Proxy.

'At this I was confused. I had never heard of this before. But when I looked it up I was horrified to see that people thought I was capable of this though to me it also explained the way I and my son had been treated at times, which I had put down to people being over-zealous in their jobs or even paranoid. But now I knew – they thought I was unfit to be a parent.

'While I was horrified, I was not overly concerned because I was still trusting the system. Also, I knew that I hadn't made anything up and it had all happened, so there was no danger of my family being split because not only had there not been any wrongdoing, there was not even anything that you could call evidence of wrongdoing.

'After her visit, the Department of Family Services worker said to me that she felt her time had been totally wasted because as far as she was concerned there was no evidence of Munchausen Syndrome or Munchausen Syndrome by Proxy, but I did not know if I was still being investigated or not and I had not known before the worker told me that I was being investigated.'

While the Department of Family Services worker may have felt there was not enough evidence of either MSBP or Munchausen Syndrome, in many ways the damage had been done because the accusation was on her medical records.

Tammie still trusted the system and thought that she would be OK as she had been cleared of suffering from MSBP and therefore the accusation would simply be removed from her records. Not so.

It was then that Tammie discovered that even though medical professionals say they do all they can to remain neutral and observant of only the facts, the accusation that this woman was a bad mother who harmed her child was one that brought out emotions in people – emotions that clouded the facts.

'The minute that term went on my medical records, the damage was done.

'Whenever I saw the Munchausen phrase on my records I tried

to set the record straight with staff but they just fobbed me off because it seems that when you are accused of it they automatically assume you are a pathological liar, even when you have evidence to the contrary.

'The minute the phrase is spotted or mentioned you are fighting a losing battle. One facility tried to have Matthew removed from my custody based on old medical records, which had Munchausen on them. I was also told at another establishment that I would have to get the therapist's permission to talk to or visit my son.'

While the mother was being accused of psychological disorders, Matthew was being examined for Foetal Alcohol Syndrome by a geneticist. While this was ruled out, the expert could not rule out Foetal Alcohol Effects, which is an entirely different thing.

The now seven-year-old Matthew was calmer than he had been for a few years, being a normal child, but as he neared his eighth birthday he started to regress, for no obvious reason.

'People started noticing a pattern of behaviour where he would push out his bedroom screen and jump out the window and disappear. He also started to take bikes that were lying around.

'On top of this, he started telling enormous tall tales and believed that he couldn't be hurt or get caught because he was, as he put it, "smarter than the cops". I tried everything, reading any book that I thought might have something – no matter how tenuous – that could help me.

'The accusations of MSBP also played a part in this, with my accusers being convinced that I had "triggered" my son's problems and that if I were just a better parent that he would be fine.

'Things were so bad that I was starting to agree with them at times, but fighting them and looking after Matthew were taking their toll on me and it became obvious that I could not look after him properly, keeping him safe.

'His case manager recommended hospitalisation, and I finally agreed.

'But while he was hospitalised, I started to gather my strength and started researching to see what could be done, not only for his condition, but also to keep us close as a family.

'I started hitting Internet sites like Momabear's Place and www.conductdisorders.com and started asking questions.

'As I said, I was starting to believe that I was a bad parent, so discovering sites like this kept me sane. I had been racked with guilt until I found out that I was not alone, that there were – and are – thousands of kids like this and thousands of parents like me!

'I cried with relief on and off for two days! But this relief was tinged with sadness as I knew that others were suffering and being falsely accused the way I was.'

While Matthew was in hospital, a chance meeting with a member of Matthew's birth family revealed important details that could have saved a lot of problems and heartbreak seven years earlier.

'The woman from the maternal birth family let us in on the fact that mental illness and alcoholism runs through her family, including birth mom, both grandparents and an uncle.

'From other details that she told me, Matthew and his mother – when she was the same age – acted almost identically, but therapies and medical theories had changed in between.

'I also learnt that although it was true the guy from high school had heard my hubby and I had lost a child before he asked us if we would like to adopt, they had been told they weren't being allowed to keep the baby because the birth mother had previously lost custody of three other children for neglect.'

For Tammie, this opened up new avenues of treating her son and changed so much, but it would not have changed her adopting Matthew in the first place.

'If we had known this earlier it could and would have made such a difference, but it would not have stopped me taking him. I fell in love with this child the first time his birth mother let me feel him move within her. He had my heart before he was even born, but so much pain could have been avoided and so much harm averted if we had had some more details.'

When he came out of hospital, Tammie felt there was such a difference in him and she was able to enjoy being with her son for the first time in ages. She felt she had her little boy back.

'He was almost as relaxed and happy as I was. He wasn't running all over the place. He was walking to and from the school bus, trying hard at school and being a normal seven-year-old, but like before, it didn't last.'

As Matthew's self-esteem started to fall, his misbehaviour started to rise and he was acting up at school, showing signs of telling tales, hypersexuality and running away from classes.

Tammie did not discover this right away as he was only acting up away from home, but when his behaviour became too bad, doctors suggested another period of hospitalisation. But what had worked before, did not work this time. Neither did altering his medication.

One other thing was changed to suit Matthew's moods – his education. After an independent evaluation, he was placed in an appropriate special education classroom, which has helped calm him down, but he still has problems. The accusations of MSBP on the medical report remained and it was not until 2000 that everything came together and paediatricians realised what was wrong with Matthew.

Unfortunately, it would take one of his worst-ever attacks in April that year to make this happen. The shock for Tammie of what her son did pales in comparison with the shock of what happened next.

'He ran away from the bus stop, stole a bike and a toy from Kmart, and tried to talk a clerk at the Greyhound depot into letting him get on the bus.

'Police officers brought him home and I was really angry with him for what he had done. The officers left and as I was chewing his butt for that morning's episode, he practically exploded!

'Foul words were not the only things thrown at me as he was throwing pictures and a magazine rack, hitting me with his fists, but then it got worse. I was calling the officers back to help me when he managed to get a hold of a piece of string and he tried to garrotte himself with it.

'When the officer arrived she called for an ambulance on her radio – she couldn't use my phone as he had it already and because it took both of us to take him down, preventing him from banging his head on the floor and biting me.

'That night, we spent six hours in the Emergency Room with a police guard. My son's therapeutic aide, case manager, aunt and I all took turns with him so he didn't hurt himself or anyone else. He threatened to shoot the nurse in the face if he got hold of the cop's gun.

'Over the course of those six hours he alternated between the rages and deep, gut-wrenching remorseful sobs that would've ripped out the heart of any mother who cared for her child.

'When he was raging, he'd cry, "I want my mom", whether it was me holding him or not, but when he sobbed he'd cling to me, begging forgiveness. In an effort to help, they gave him 3 mg of IM Ativan and 100 mg of Benadryl, which is enough to knock an adult out, but both barely phased him other than to slow him down a little.'

He was eventually moved out of the ER and Tammie was given a choice of letting him go home or placing him in a care hospital. Unfortunately the only bed available in the entire state at the time was in a hospital with a bad reputation, where two children had committed suicide the year before, but Tammie reluctantly felt she had no choice but to admit him as she knew she could not take him as he was.

Hindsight, though, has changed Tammie's mind.

'In retrospect, I should have taken him home. He wouldn't have been abused at home.

'He was only there three weeks before someone who was obviously not trained took him down, football-tackle style. They knelt on his upper back and grabbed his legs, which ground his face into the carpet and gave him a good-sized rug burn right next to his eye.

'When I complained, I was patronised and assured that it had been "taken care of" in house. Scared to death for my child, I called the doctor to ask what his treatment plan was and was told he would not discuss it with me, that my son was in more danger in my care than his.

'I immediately tried to remove him and was thwarted. Truly scared to death now, his case manager and I went up the following Monday and removed him. As unstable as my son was, there was no way I was going to allow someone like that access to my little boy.

'We waited for a month with stepped-up services and very little sleep until a bed became available in an acceptable facility. He went there in June 2000 and has been there ever since.'

It was there that Tammie and her family discovered what is wrong with Matthew.

'According to doctors he may be suffering from Oppositional Defiant Disorder and Bipolar Syndrome. ODD is a psychiatric disorder that is characterised by aggressiveness and a tendency to purposefully bother and irritate others.

'It was felt that he may also be suffering from – and some tried to treat him for – Attention Deficit Hyperactivity Disorder, but we later worked out that he had Bipolar Disorder, which is a well-known and extremely serious psychiatric disorder that normally occurs in late adolescence and adulthood, but in the past decade its existence in childhood and early adolescence has been revealed. Most clinicians are ill prepared to recognise children with Bipolar Disorder and parents have no information available to them. The disorder most commonly confused with Bipolar Disorder is ADHD, but there are subtle distinctions that an expert should spot, if they are properly looking for ADHD or Bipolar Disorder and not just ADHD as so many do. While the symptoms may be similar, the treatments are not.'

Tammie, like many other people accused of MSBP, found that she had been accused of something because of her son's condition. She later learnt from others accused that children with ADHD, ODD and Bipolar Disorder very often have parents accused of MSBP.

After being accused of being more harmful for her son than the home he was in, she fought to get the references to MSBP removed from her records.

According to the Director of the Department of Family Services they have now been removed, with the charge against her being put down as unsubstantiated and the file on it closed. The phrase remains on Matthew's records though and no one has ever apologised to Tammie for the false accusations.

After her ordeal, Tammie is unsure if there is such a condition as MSBP. What worries her is the way the medical community uses the tag without being certain either.

'Do I believe in Munchausen Syndrome by Proxy after all I have been through?

'I don't know. What I do believe is that if this condition truly exists it is as overdiagnosed and abused as the label ADHD is. The accusers need to be more careful and be held accountable if they make a mistake.'

While it would be nice to hope for a happy ending for the mother and son, Tammie knows she may never have the easy days that other parents have, but that does not diminish her love for Matthew because at least they can have a future together.

'Matthew is now on Tegretol. He has had one wonderful home visit without any problems. He has his good days and his bad days but we are coping and we are trying. Just now, the plan for the future is to make sure he's stable.

'I don't know what the future holds for us. I'm 35 now and both my son and I have had to endure a lot to get this far. He still goes back and forth between stability and teetering on the edge, but I know adult Bipolars that are leading productive, positive lives with treatment.

'Right now I just want him to be able to enjoy being a kid. We played catch-up in a big way this summer, and he had a great time. He's up to date with his class, he loves Britney Spears and N'Sync, plays soccer, skateboards, rollerblades and is in Cub Scouts and will soon be in Tai Kwon Do. He's just a neat kid! My kid!

'But I know we are in for some tough times ahead. Mention of MSBP remains in my son's medical records and they refuse to remove or refute it in any way. In nine years my child will be an adult and this will not affect me at all, but unless it is fixed in his records, it will follow my son for the rest of his life and I fear that if that is the case his life may not be long.

'My biggest fear is that someone will see that, deny him treatment and that he'll commit suicide. My son is manic depressive, which turns out to be rampant in his birth family, and nearly one-fifth of all Bipolars commit suicide if untreated. To make matters worse, the suicide rate in the state where I live is extremely high among adolescent males. We are fourth in the nation for suicides.

'But I hope we can get through the tough times. I'm not going to let him down now. We are a family.'

Twelve

The Future

Having looked at the past of MSBP and where it is now, it is only right to ask what future it has. As we have seen it has blossomed like a nuclear missile's mushroom cloud over the past decade – will the coming years see things get worse, with more people being accused of it or will informed opinion decide that there is no such thing?

Brian Morgan thinks the future is bright for those who have campaigned against the false allegations.

'There's light at the end of the tunnel within the next few years. I think that with the attention that has been given to Southall over some of the things he has done and Sir Roy rarely defending his work, I think it will start to die a death.

'If you look at it there are no upcoming medical experts saying that MSBP has any credence to it. There are no new champions for the condition and without medical experts to back it up and fight for it, it will go away, perhaps to the extent of being discredited.

'Hopefully the end will happen sooner rather than later and the suffering of those who have been falsely accused will come to an end.

'In my opinion the tide is turning and it is turning quickly. Don't get me wrong, I'm not saying that some of the people accused are not ill in some form or other, but I believe the next few years will see clarity and sense come through with regard to MSBP and some other controversial conditions.'

Others share Morgan's optimism. Stuart Carnie said: 'People are questioning the doctors more and more; there is less blind acceptance of what one doctor will say. In many ways that is sad because it could undermine the doctor/patient relationship, but if that is being abused by doctors in the first place then perhaps this is a good thing.

'A lot of change could be brought about by the simple fact of doctors being more able to readily admit when they don't know what a diagnosis may be. Better to be honest and say, "I don't know" than to stomp about accusing people of being Munch mothers because that fits the fact that you can't explain any other way.

'Sherlock Holmes may have said that once you eliminate everything on the basis of the evidence you then have whatever you are left with – no matter how unlikely, it is the only explanation – but that's not the case in medicine. There are illnesses and ailments that we don't yet know about. Doctors, despite the God complex some of them have, do not know everything. Perhaps doctors gaining some humility would be a welcome first step in the process of doing away with MSBP.

'I aim to be involved in the fight against MSBP. In July 2001 I fled the UK to South America to continue in trying to highlight the injustices involved.

'Yes, I left the country to avoid being put in jail for my part in trying to help an MSBP-accused family but I felt that the only way to get justice was to fight from a position of strength and not from a prison cell.

'What we did was for the best reason in the world, to protect the child from the real danger of abuse in social services.

'I know that no publication can say too much for legal reasons but I maintain that the whole case against us was flawed. I was told by the police at one point that no criminal offence had taken place and all they were looking at was a child missing from home. There also seemed to be problems with the family introducing medical evidence.

'I was shocked to find out that the child's mother and grandmother have been sent to prison for nine months and the child's father for six months. What kind of society do we live in when the courts can lock parents up for trying to protect their child from harm?'

Penny Mellor hopes that not only will the parents find respite from the accusations of MSBP, but also that the medical staff who have pursued the allegations will be investigated by the police.

'Make no mistake here,' she said, 'there are medical staff who deserve to be investigated for either their methods or the way in which they have pursued parents. Just turning round and suddenly saying, "Oh sorry, we don't think there is such a thing as MSBP" is not going to be good enough. Doctors and medical experts have to be held accountable for their actions and also for the harm that they have caused to families. There may even be calls to see if children have died or been injured because of the wrongful diagnoses by doctors.

'Then, once that is done, we have to look at the possibility of compensation for those who have been falsely accused. Too much damage has been done for it just to be all swept under the carpet and just ignored, which all too often is the way the British establishment likes to deal with things. This time, that can't be allowed to happen if MSBP is blown open for what it is.

'And after that, we have to look at the possibility of seeing what other fictitious illnesses and accusations there are.

'If the medical community says one day that there is no such thing as MSBP but suddenly turns round with a new theory that is the same with a different name, then nothing has been achieved. There has to be clarity and more independent assessment of the medical experts.'

Retired lawyer Martin Knowles thinks the recent incorporation of the European Convention on Human Rights into UK law will play a major role in MSBP in the future.

'When you look at it, there are a number of articles that can be used to help parents accused. For a start there is Article 8, which guarantees that everyone has the right to respect for his private and family life, his home and his correspondence. A good lawyer could argue that their MSBP-accused client is having their privacy invaded.

'There might even be grounds for Article 3, which states that no one shall be subjected to torture or to inhuman or degrading treatment or punishment. Some parents might argue that they have been degraded by their treatment at the hands of police or medical staff.

'Then there is Article 5, which states that everyone has the right to liberty and security of person, except in a number of circumstances including the lawful detention of a person after conviction by a competent court. Parents might argue that the court is not competently qualified in the matters surrounding MSBP to make a judgment. Using this would also require the people involved to have something against the expert witnesses to introduce doubt as to their credibility, but that could be done.

'Again, Article 6, which allows for the entitlement of a fair and public hearing within a reasonable time by an independent and impartial tribunal established by law, could be used in a similar fashion.

'With regards to media being banned from giving publicity to MSBP trials, Article 10 can be used, as it reads "everyone has the right to freedom of expression. This right shall include freedom to hold opinions and to receive and impart information and ideas without interference by public authority and regardless of frontiers". Of course the authorities can use a section of Article 6 against this one, as it states, after going on about fair judgment, that "judgment shall be pronounced publicly but the press and public may be excluded from all or part of the trial in the interests of morals... where the interests of juveniles or the protection of the private life of the parties so require".

'Then lastly, there would be Article 17, which states that no one can try and set out to destroy the rights which are enshrined in the European Convention on Human Rights.

'As I say, a good lawyer could tie a court up with most, if not all of these. And while the prosecuting side may want to go ahead with the trial anyway, it may get to the point where this sort of prosecution is not cost-efficient, especially if witnesses are being discredited, which could affect future cases.

'As more lawyers become aware of the full potential that the European Convention on Human Rights gives them, I think we will see challenges along the lines that I have laid out.'

However, not everyone is convinced that MSBP will be abolished or discredited in the future.

Dr Mark Stuartson thinks it may well be quite the opposite.

'I've never been for or against MSBP. It's an area that I keep a very open mind about, but over the coming years we might see more tests being developed that show there is such a thing.

'I think it's too early to say that genetics might one day show us if there is such a thing as a genetic predisposition towards something like MSBP – and if there is, it will no doubt be called the Allitt or Bush gene, regardless of how accurate that label would be – but there might be more advanced screening and psychological tests that would help us identify those who suffer from MSBP. There may also be some forms of treatment developed for them, a form of Prozac which controls their less desirable impulses, but I would imagine this would only be used in conjunction with psychotherapy.'

Indeed, psychologist Maria Enton believes that her area may provide the biggest breakthroughs in MSBP.

'We are learning more and more about behaviour and the human brain all the time and there is no reason for this learning to decrease instead of increase.

'We may be able to pinpoint what it is that causes Munchausen Syndrome, MSBP and other conditions like it. Once we can do that, we can start to look at treatments and potential cures.

'Like so many other mental illnesses, which is what I think MSBP is, we have to understand the human mind and the illness before we can start to look at treatment.

'That is something else that may also happen in the future – clarification about MSBP being a mental or physical condition.

That should be one of the first steps, with international bodies getting together to sort it out.'

One doctor who has worked with Roy Meadow, but who asked not to be named, said there was an infinite number of possibilities as to what might happen next.

She said: 'Obviously, it's a very polarised debate, with the pro- and anti-MSBP camps, with neither giving way to the other. But instead of the condition being proven once and for all or it being discredited once and for all, what you may find is that the phrase itself drops out of use and is replaced by something else.

'As others have noted, MSBP is a very emotive phrase and that has not been helped by the media exposure given to it. What we may want to look at is having no phrasing at all and just saying what people do to others.

'From that we can then look at seeing if there is any common ground. Are the adults involved suffering from some form of stress, possibly a form of post-natal depression and it is this which is causing the injuries, or is there more to it? At the most basic level, it could be argued that MSBP is just a form of depression or stress and it is the outlet for that person's suffering which is unique, ie they transfer it onto children.

'After all, if the point of MSBP is to draw attention to yourself as a cry for help, then it certainly fits the bill of some existing conditions and depressions. The person is basically crying for help. What makes it unique is the way in which the person cries for help.

'It's an area that still needs further work to examine what the position is at the moment, but those coming into it should be vetted to ensure that they have no preconceived notions. Coming into something like this with preconceived notions could jeopardise their findings or have them accused of bias.

'But what we have to remember here is that children have been, and are being, harmed – killed, even – and that is what we are trying to prevent.

'In an attempt to placate the anti-MSBP groups I would also have the authorities look into the possibilities of more examining of doctors in cases where MSBP is alleged. This second group could then help to clear the doctors and medical staff of any perceived wrongdoing, pointing out that there is something wrong with the child and that it is not just a misdiagnosis.

'As well as showing the protesters that the doctor is not in the wrong, it would also be a form of reassurance for the medical staff, who would have been cleared of wrongdoing and also been backed up by their superiors.

'But it's not just going to go away. Nothing in the medical world ever does.'

What the future holds for MSBP is uncertain. As has been pointed out, there may be breakthroughs that either pinpoint the causes of it or discredit it, or it may be renamed.

Only one thing is certain. For the next few years at least parents will continue to be suspected at times by doctors when they come in with injured children whose injuries clear up when the parents are not around, or who have symptoms that are inexplicable. And that will lead to families being split up and doctors having allegations and rumours spread about their professional abilities and private lives. Regardless of what the future holds, the suffering continues for now.

Thirteen

Martine, England

As this book has shown so far, being accused of MSBP once is traumatic for the families involved, but some families have had to go through the hell of being called dangerous parents more than once.

Martine Davids has had to go through the ordeal twice and now knows that if anything else ever happens to her children, the likelihood is that she will lose them for ever.

Martine and her husband Peter were both 24 when she first fell pregnant in the second year of their marriage. Excited, the family picked the names Angela and Paul, depending on the sex of the baby.

But in the second month of pregnancy, Martine miscarried. No reason for the loss was ever given. In the words of their doctor, 'It just wasn't meant to be.'

The couple grieved for a long time, with what would have been the birth date being an incredibly traumatic time.

Peter remembers: 'It was November 1994. We had been planning to leave England before the news of the pregnancy and after we lost Angela or Paul we decided to put it off for a while.

'We couldn't get our heads round anything at first. We would look at other people who had kids and wonder why ours was dead and theirs wasn't. We would avoid friends who had children. We were bitter.

'Looking back we're ashamed of the way we felt, but I was told that it was more or less natural for couples who have suffered miscarriages to be like this and being bitter is part of the whole healing process.'

The couple got through the tragedy and the first anniversary of what would have been the birth. As the New Year of 1996 swept in, they decided that instead of emigrating, they would just do some travelling to help them get over everything that had happened.

Six months later, after touring India, the Middle East and the Far East, they returned home to settle down in the south of England.

Not long after coming home, the couple found that Martine was pregnant again. While overjoyed, they were also terrified. Martine could not help but worry. However, stressing her system out was not good for her unborn child.

Peter wanted her to quit her job immediately.

'We still had some money so we could have got by. I was able to work from home a lot, which meant I would be able to look after her.

'I don't deny that I would have completely spoiled her. I had gone off the idea of having a child, but when Martine fell pregnant again, I was excited and hoped that this time we would have a baby.

'Martine worked for the first two months, but after that I insisted she stop and she agreed. I also started working from home full time, up until the first trimester was passed.

'People were wondering why she was off [work], but it was put down to stress-related illness. It wasn't because of nastiness we weren't telling. We just didn't want to jinx it.

'I didn't feel good about telling the lie, but it was a lot easier than telling people she was pregnant. That wasn't the problem. I was more worried about what would happen if she lost the baby again.'

At six months, it was becoming obvious to a lot of people what was really happening, so the couple came clean about it all.

'There was a lot of relief that day and most people automatically understood why we hadn't mentioned anything. No one fell out with us over it, but I must admit to being concerned about the amount of fussing that was going on with regard to Martine. Not because of any male notions of being left out or not being the centre of attention. Far from it. I just didn't want her left too tired. At times my fussing started to come between us.'

Martine is less diplomatic about that time. 'We were arguing constantly. He wouldn't let me do anything. If he had been able to get it all his own way he would have had me sitting on a chair for nine months, never moving at all.

'Don't get me wrong, I knew what he was trying to do, but it was really suffocating me. At some points he was the most stressful thing during the pregnancy.'

The nine months were fairly trouble-free with just the odd scare, mostly when Martine would slip or fall and Peter would have her halfway to the local hospital before he would believe her insistence that she was OK and there was no need to worry.

The birth itself was, according to the doctor, fairly routine and straightforward, with Peter Jr coming into the world weighing 7 lb 4 oz.

According to Martine, it was hell on earth. 'All that miracle of birth stuff they tell you is absolute nonsense. It was like shitting a bowling ball and while it's nice to see your child at the end of it all, it doesn't make up for the pain of during it.

'After Peter was born, I was worried as he was very quiet, but the doctor gave him a few taps and he made really quiet little screams. I just burst into tears with relief that he seemed OK, but some of the tears were also just relief that it was all over.

The happy father wasn't there at the birth. 'I'd chatted it over with the doctor and a few others and we came to the realisation that I would only be in the way, especially if she was in pain, as I would be fussing, trying to get that sorted. The doctor had warned me that if I tried that he'd have me anaesthetised. I don't think he was kidding either.'

After the first few days, the parents were told that they had a normal baby boy, complete with black hair and blue eyes. The only problem seemed to be that he was very, very quiet.

Doctors and nurses told the new parents not to worry about this. Yes, he was a small baby and yes, he did appear to have small lungs but it was not a major issue. The lungs seemed to be working normally and all his vocal equipment was there, so there was no need for concern.

If anything, people quipped, this could mean a baby who was quiet at nights, which would let them get a full night's sleep. Peter never saw it that way. He was trying to work out if he could work at night in the same room as Peter Jr so he could keep his eye on him and make sure he was breathing.

'I know it sounds incredibly paranoid, but I was terrified at the time for a number of reasons.

'First off, the thought of cot death had been preying on my mind more or less constantly since the baby was born, so if I was in the same room and awake, working, it would mean that I could be nearer him to react.

'I was thinking the same with regard to if he had any breathing problems. I would be there, awake, so I could constantly check on him.

'Some people, including my dad, said I was being too paranoid, but I said to them that I would rather be too paranoid and on alert in case something happened instead of being relaxed and then blaming myself for years if anything did go wrong.'

When the family came home, Peter made the arrangements. Their spare room was converted into a half-study, complete with computer, fax and all the other equipment he thought he needed to be a successful nocturnal freelance journalist. The other half of the room was converted into a nursery and play area for his smaller namesake.

The arrangement was that he would go to bed with Martine, stay there until she fell asleep and then go next door and work away on whatever he was doing, while keeping an ear out for his son.

'People asked me how I would be able to do that, but I was working without wearing headphones – something I resented at first – but once you got used to hearing Peter's breathing in the background, then any time it wasn't there you would notice it instantly.

'It's like the noise of a ticking grandfather clock. You don't really notice it in the background, but once the clock stops you notice it instantly.

'He was fine most nights – he would stop the odd time just for gurgling noises.

'It was a bit of a panic before I got settled into a routine, as any time I thought his regular breathing was stopping I'd jump out the chair and run over to his cot, making so much noise that I'd wake him up. I eventually rearranged the office so that he was to the side of me when I was working. I had been worried that the tapping of the keys would keep him awake, but the rhythm seemed to help him sleep, not that he needed much help as he slept constantly.

'That didn't worry me though, as Martine had told me that all the babies in her family were very heavy sleepers.'

As the months went on, the routine continued and there were no worries about how the family were getting on. Peter and Martine still spent time together. Martine went back on her promise of going back to work at the bank, instead admitting that she had just said that so she could get the maternity leave, but things were going well for the family.

Martine's mother, Julia, was only concerned about one thing. 'By the time younger Peter was nine months old, Peter and Martine had not had a night to themselves since the birth. There was always one of them with him.

'I found this quite worrying, as I don't think it does anyone any good to be cooped up like that. Peter admitted to me once that his thinking round it was that Martine at times confided she was worried someone would steal the baby or it would die, so she wanted to spend all her time with him.

'Given the miscarriage I could see where the feeling for that was coming from, but I was determined that they start to get some more time on their own.'

That was not to happen.

One night Peter picked up his son, who had woken up. He was still very quiet and Peter was tickling his belly when he suddenly flopped out, like a starfish held upside down.

Peter said his heart stopped: 'I almost dropped him with fright. One moment he was trying to grab my hand, which was tickling him, the next moment his eyes rolled up and he just went lifeless.

'I grabbed the phone that was on my desk and dialled 999. I then shouted at Martine to wake up and as she was doing that I phoned the local hospital.

'I know it sounds strange, but I had run over in my head what I would do if something went wrong so many times that it seemed like second nature to me.'

The ambulance came and Peter Jr was rushed to hospital. On the way to the hospital he came back round, much to everyone's relief, and then became lifeless again.

The paramedics tried to calm the frantic parents by pointing out to them that their child was alive – in fact there didn't seem to be anything drastically wrong with his vital signs. They were a little under normal, but that was all.

At the hospital, the doctors ran a number of tests. A specialist consultant was brought in to run more tests, and as the tests increased so did the stress levels of the parents.

'Martine was bouncing off the walls. She was angry that she didn't know what was going on and she kept quizzing me as to what had happened in the room. She kept going over and over it, as if she was trying to catch me out.

'What didn't help was that I knew some of the doctors and staff through one of my old jobs when I had been the reporter for all that was happening at the hospital.

'They kept coming over and telling me that they were doing more tests, nothing else. However, Martine seemed to have difficulty in believing this and started accusing me of hiding the truth from her, which I wasn't. I was in the dark about it as much as she was, and if truth be told I was starting to get really angry with her accusations that this was somehow all my fault.'

The consultant came back to them with some good and bad news. Peter was fine, but they thought that he may have some form of epilepsy, and it would take more tests to find out for sure.

According to the consultant, what they thought was happening was that Peter was having mini-fits that were leaving him exhausted and making him pass out.

'The consultant said that it was very possible that the flopping, which I had assumed was him passing out,' remembers Peter, 'was actually just a reflex at the end of the mini-fit. The consultant also thought it was possible that Peter was never awake at all. It was more a case of I had seen his eyes moving about, just like adults do in REM sleep, and his eyelids flickering, so I thought he was awake.

'He was never awake and passing out, he was just having little fits in his sleep.'

The parents were worried about giving their 10-month-old child any amount of drugs. Part of them wanted to wait until all the test results were returned – but they had no patience at all for this. They wanted to know what was wrong with their son. Yesterday.

For Peter it was an agonising time. 'I would watch him and worry every time he flopped. If I thought it was a bad fit I would get him straight to the hospital, not always stopping to wake Martine.'

However, it was Martine who found one way around constant fretting about the fits. She found that tickling Peter Jr's tummy or shaking him during them made him wake up, and while he was still fitting, at least they knew he was awake.

The doctor also told the parents that the fits were not fits in any technical sense. They were more like spasms or twitches. While the words may have been different, the parents still panicked and it got to the point where the doctor had to put his foot down.

Martine remembers that they were asked to attend the doctor's office one day.

'We were wondering what it was about, though we hoped they had pinpointed what was up with Peter.

'When we got there, he told us that we had to stop being so possessive and paranoid over Peter Jr.

'He pointed out that for the last three months the hospital was seeing the family at least once every fortnight during the nights, sometimes more.

'He told us that we should see if it developed into a waking form of epilepsy or if he was just having sleeping twitches, something he might grow out of.

'I wasn't happy with what he told us and I said that I was taking Peter to another hospital for a second opinion. We told him that if things were bad, we could take bad news.

'We ended up agreeing on a compromise. He would allow Peter to be looked at by other doctors except the ones in their hospital and his GP if, at the end of it all, the family remained with him and we accepted whatever the other doctors said.

'He said he would also abide by whatever the doctors found as long as it did not compromise him ethically. A strange thing for him to say, but I just thought that was him covering his back.'

The couple sought the second opinion, getting another hospital to run exhaustive tests. They found no sign of epilepsy, but couldn't find anything else wrong with him either, but according to Peter and Martine the fits continued, as did the call-outs for ambulances.

'At one point,' Martine remembers, 'someone joked that we were on first name terms with most of the paramedics and also the hospital staff, which I didn't find funny because it was actually true.

'I wasn't in the mood to be funny as I just wanted to know what was up with my son.

'What the paramedics did agree with us on was that it was exhausting. On more than one occasion, the paramedics said to us that they didn't know how we were keeping going doing this. It wasn't meant as a criticism, more just a statement that we were running ourselves into the ground.'

When they went back to the doctor, he said that nothing had been found to be wrong with Peter but that he had managed to arrange for a paediatrician at a London hospital to look at him.

The family travelled to London and over the course of a few days brain scans and tests were carried out on the baby. As the parents waited to get the results from the paediatrician, their hopes grew that finally they would find out what was wrong with their son and be able to move on with their lives.

After a month, the hospital doctor asked them to come in to discuss certain matters.

Believing this would be it, the beginning of the end of their troubles, instead of the beginning of them, they eagerly counted the days until the meeting. They were an hour early for it, they were so keen.

The doctor was there as well as three others that Martine and Peter did not recognise. They assumed that they were either assistants to the paediatrician or new specialists brought in.

They were neither.

The doctor calmly explained to them that the paediatrician's report said nothing was wrong with Peter Jr – all the scans and tests had been returned negative. As far as they could tell, he was a normal baby.

One of the supposed specialists then turned round and said to the parents: 'He is perfectly normal. There has never been anything wrong with him, and we think it is you who needs help. We think you may suffer from a condition known as Munchausen Syndrome by Proxy.'

For the family, this was ludicrous beyond belief. Martine burst into tears at the accusation. 'I just couldn't believe it. I thought we'd been through enough.

'I was thinking that going to the doctor's that day would have cleared up the problems with Peter Jr and that was going to be the beginning of the rest of our lives. I didn't expect things to get worse.

'Years later Peter was able to joke that when things were at the worst we should have listened to the old-fashioned country-and-western albums, where every story was a sob story. Peter said that what those people were going through would have been light relief for us compared to what was happening to us.

'But I wasn't in the mood for laughing the day we were told we were bad parents.'

Martine actually knew what MSBP was, having discovered it in a magazine article. 'I wasn't an expert on it or anything, but I knew the basics, that it came about from parents being accused of harming their children in an attempt to get attention for themselves.

'I always thought it would be something like parents putting bits of powdered glass into children's meals or keeping them awake at night with noise, things that would be easily sorted out and found.

'To be accused of it though totally shocked me. All I kept thinking was, I'm not like the mums that have been accused. I wouldn't harm my child but there I was, being accused of it.'

Peter was just stunned. 'I couldn't tell if we were both being accused or if it was just one of us. They then went on to ask us a few questions.

'They asked us who had discovered Peter Jr when he wasn't well, who had called the ambulances, what we fed him. They were really thorough.

'It got to the point that I stood up and shouted at them, "What the hell are you planning to do with these trumped-up accusations?" I had gone from being shocked to being raging.'

One of the supposed specialists, who were in fact social workers, replied, very calmly, that they would have someone accompany the family home and assess the situation there. They were also in the process of getting court approval to remove Peter Jr from his home, as they felt that would be the best move for his safety.

Unknown to the family, the court order was at a very advanced stage. When they did find out about it, they had less than one week to find a solicitor and prepare to fight the action.

The court case was simple enough: the state wanted to take the child into care for its own protection. Any matter of charges against the parents for cruelty would be a separate matter for the courts and authorities to deal with.

Peter remembers it all too well. 'We never had a chance. They had doctors and social workers to back up their argument, while our lawyer was struggling to even accept what the case was about, as he had no medical knowledge whatsoever.

'It was pretty much an open and shut case. They argued that according to the evidence they had we were putting our child at risk. We had nothing to counter this, except for the claim that we didn't do it. Being innocent until proven guilty never really got us far that day, as the judge ruled that it was in the child's best interest to be taken away from us.

'If I was a neutral I would probably have made the same decision because they had a lot of evidence and theory where we had nothing.

'The judge ruled that Peter Jr should be taken into care, but monitored to see if he had any incidents. We were also told that we would have supervised visits once a fortnight, which was something, but to have your child taken away is a bitter pill to swallow, no matter how they try to sweeten it with promises of visits.'

Over the next few weeks, Martine went through what she calls 'a personal hell', blaming herself for what had happened with both children.

'It sounds irrational now, I know, but it was the case that I was convinced that I must have done something for the loss of the first child and now I had done something that was causing me to lose the second. Even if it wasn't something like MSBP, I was thinking there must be something in my genes that made my children not well and was then destined to be a bad parent.

'Peter was very sympathetic and told me to stop being so stupid about it all as it was nothing to do with me. He – and the rest of my family – were all telling me that it was a mistake on the doctor's behalf, not my fault.

'I must have been a poor partner at that time as I was just a complete wreck again, but he took it all the time.'

Peter said it was definitely a case of keeping a stiff upper lip. 'I was angry and frustrated but I knew that the first step to getting Peter back was by showing that we were a normal family, so I had to encourage Martine to come back from her depression. In my own way I was viewing it as a war, one where it was us against the people who were trying to steal our baby.

'It sounds ridiculous and over the top to describe it that way, but at the time that was how I was looking at it. Us v Them. All I was concerning myself with was looking after Peter and Martine, getting us back together as a family.'

The three-month period also gave the lawyer a chance to start studying the topic and gaining some knowledge about it.

According to Peter, the lawyer felt the best argument was to show that while the doctors could not prove an illness, they also could not prove any harm was being caused by the parents. He was also prepared to call in all the medical experts to see what they said on the matter, knowing full well that only one of them had a theory about what might be wrong with young Peter.

The lawyer felt that the overwhelming fact that the doctors did not know if anything was wrong would work in their favour. The argument was to be that just because the doctors could not find anything wrong with Peter Jr, it did not mean that there was nothing wrong with him.

He was also going to try a more risky tactic – videoing Peter Jr while he slept.

The social workers were reluctant to allow this at first, but when they were promised that the videotape would not only be on every night and also when the parents visited, but that they could use the tape as evidence as well, they agreed to it.

After their first visit to the social work home together, Peter made the trips himself because Martine found them too distressing.

'I knew I had to try and put on a brave face, but I just couldn't do it. He seemed in good enough spirits when we visited but leaving him there was the hardest thing I had ever done. It was even worse than having to accept that I had had a miscarriage. To see my baby boy and then leave him behind was beyond cruelty in my opinion.'

As the three-month hearing approached, the family were feeling confident.

Peter and the lawyer had seen tapes that showed Peter Jr having similar episodes to before on a number of nights without any intervention from social workers, home staff or the parents. They had not told Martine of this because they felt she would worry about the attacks. Peter was also worried, but was starting to think that perhaps they were more normal than they had thought.

Come the case, the parents were told in advance that the social workers had come to the same conclusion as the lawyer and Peter, but that they still wanted some medical evidence before they would release the child.

The following hours were among the most nerve-racking for the parents.

Doctor after doctor said that there was no proof that Peter Jr was being harmed by the parents, but at the same time they were obliged to point out that they could not see anything medically wrong with the boy.

This went on through three doctors until the fourth stepped up and said that while he agreed with his colleagues, he also had to point out that in his opinion, Peter Jr was suffering from some form of fit in his sleep and perhaps a minor case of sleep apnoea-related passing out. He felt that the child was in no danger from his parents but would have to be regularly monitored just to make sure he was fine. He also thought it would be prudent to examine the child's lungs and breathing passages just to make sure there was no obstruction.

The judge agreed, but added that he wanted the parents to have some form of visitor from social services to try to calm them down instead of panicking any time their child was injured or appeared to be injured.

However, the lawyer was told that the accusation of MSBP could not be removed from the medical files at that hearing. That would take another hearing.

The family, at that moment, did not care. They were to be reunited and they did not mind the fact that someone would be keeping an eye on them for a while.

According to Martine, 'The thought of someone keeping an eye on us – which in effect was what was happening – did not bother us as we were just so happy to have Peter Jr back. That was all that mattered.'

As the years went on, trying to get MSBP removed from the medical records faded into the background as the family got on with the normal business of living life. Martine went back to work as Peter turned two years old, while Daddy stayed at home and learned how to juggle a comfortable freelance journalist lifestyle with that of a househusband and father.

Peter Jr continued to have what were dubbed micro-fits in his sleep, but his parents worried about them less and less, especially after he had some minor work carried out on his nose to free up his breathing.

The years passed. Peter Jr started school, the parents put some weight on, growing content with their happy lives. The pain of the earlier years was forgotten. Martine found herself pregnant again. The family were still as cautious as they had been with Peter in admitting it, but as the end of the first trimester approached they felt secure in letting people know what was happening, and this time Martine said she would stay at her job after the pregnancy.

According to his parents, six-year-old Peter seemed to accept the fact that he would have someone keeping him company at nights fairly quickly. It did not seem to trouble him at all. What was worrying them was the possibility that this third child of theirs would suffer from the same sleeping problem as Peter Jr.

As news of the pregnancy spread, the worries of Martine and Peter did too because Peter Jr was starting to exhibit some strange behaviour. He was coming home from school with bruises and then waking up in the morning with more bruises.

When asked what had happened, Peter Jr would fake all knowledge of the bruises, even denying them when they were pointed out to him. At first it was put down to rough and tumble at his new school, but his behaviour began to get more and more erratic and he appeared to be having severe fits in the middle of the night, much more violent than anything he had ever had before.

This resulted in a number of late-night trips to the local hospital, which for Peter and Martine were all too familiar. Peter remembers: 'We were trying not to say it to each other, but we thought the doctors would start accusing Martine and myself again of bad parenting or even MSBP.'

As the weeks went on, the parents' worst fears were confirmed. They were led into a room and told that it was felt that Martine posed a danger to Peter Jr. It was insinuated that there may be some imbalance brought about by the pregnancy that was causing her to act this way. This time, Peter was accused of nothing.

The family had been preparing for this, re-enlisting the lawyer from years earlier. He told them that the first stage was going to be an order attempting to take Peter Jr into care. The lawyer said they were to fight this with an unusual approach, something that he had learned had worked in America.

The court case did indeed argue that Martine was suffering from MSBP, bringing up the previous situation and suggesting that she had some form of the condition that only manifested itself from time to time. The social workers also argued that having a lawyer ready to deal with any possible MSBP allegation showed that there was mental instability in the family because only someone paranoid would have a lawyer on standby.

When the social work department came to argue that the child had to be looked after by those who could care for it, the Davids' lawyer agreed. He then asked, who could care for a child more than Peter Jr's own father and grandmother?

He argued for Julia to move in as a nanny, while Peter was always at home already. To ensure the child's safety, mother and child were never to be left alone and videotapes were to be made of Peter Jr when sleeping. Bolts and locks that only Peter Sr could open were also to be put on doors and there would be regular visits by social workers.

It was a long string of conditions, but it worked. However, the air was heavy with threats, with the Davids left understanding that if there were any problems not only would Peter Jr be taken away, the unborn baby might be too.

Once they were allowed back home, few people visited the expectant mother. Gossip and tittle-tattle had marked her out as a bad mother.

Peter Jr's condition cleared up, though he still had bruises from school. Teachers were ordered to send home notes explaining any marks that appeared on him.

The family grew closer, the adversity bringing them together. Then one day, while they were with Julia, everything fell into place.

'I was in the back garden with Peter Jr and he was asking me why no one came round any more. I told him that because some people thought his mum was a bad mum that a lot of people didn't want to be about.

'He said mum wasn't a bad mum, but he liked it with less people about as he got more time with everyone. I just laughed as I remembered my mum telling me that after my sister was born I used to pester everyone for attention, feeling left out. I was laughing up until I remembered that I used to always graze my knees to get people's sympathy. I started to wonder if Peter had done the same.'

After a few trips to doctors, social workers and psychiatrists, the court accepted that Martine had not been harming Peter this time either. It turned out that this time round the cause of the problem was Peter Jr himself. He had been acting up in order to gain attention for himself because he was used to the fuss that he got.

When it started to lessen he tried various measures to get the attention back, measures that had all been seen by the doctors as the mother mistreating him. He had behaved when the doctors were about purely because he knew that the doctors were taking an interest in him, but also because of the reverse: he didn't want the attention of strangers, just that of the people he knew.

This type of behaviour, according to doctors, is not uncommon once a second child is born.

The accusations were dropped. Martine gave birth to a healthy baby boy, Patrick, who has had none of the breathing or fit problems of Peter Jr. Peter Jr still has small fits in his sleep but they seem to do him no harm, though doctors are investigating the possibility of some form of hyperactivity that only manifests itself in sleep.

But that is just a possibility. One thing that is certain is that Martine hopes she will never go through the accusations again. 'I know that it's there on my record that I've been investigated twice for being a mad mum and I will have to start fighting the battle to have them removed, but it's not exactly a cheap fight and there are a lot of other things money needs to be spent on. Peter is pushing for it a lot more than I am, so we'll just have to wait and see how it goes. If we get spare money then we will. I don't think it's the sort of thing that comes under the "no win, no fee" legal deals that you see on television.

'We're a family and we are together. That is what is important just now. I hope to never face accusations of being a bad parent again, but it terrifies me that I might. Call me anything you want, but don't call me a bad mother.'

Peter looks back on it all and is fairly honest in that the Davids themselves may be partially to blame. 'I often wonder how things would have turned out if Angela or Paul had been born. Would we have fussed so much? Probably not.

'I thought back at one point and wondered that perhaps the death of Angela or Paul made us so paranoid with Peter, which led to us smothering him with attention and worry as he grew up.

From that, he worked out that he could get attention through certain methods and so when he was no longer getting attention he started acting up to get the attention he wanted. You could argue that it is all our fault because Martine to this day still thinks there must have been a weakness in one of us for the miscarriage to occur.

'I confessed all of this at one point to a minister in a hospital and he said that I should not go looking to place blame or take blame. I told him I wasn't religious and wouldn't fall for the argument of God moving in mysterious ways. He replied that wasn't what he was trying to tell me. The point was that sometimes things happen that we have no control over and accepting that would be a good thing.

'At times I can accept it, other times I can't. What I can accept is that I have my family around me. A woman and two children I love. There have been painful parts to it all, but the love makes up for that and I just hope that we never have to go through anything like this again. It would seem unlikely, but I would have said that after the first time.'

Afterword

As I said at the beginning, my opinion did not come into this book. Some people who have seen early versions claim that I am more sympathetic towards the mothers and those accused than I am to the medical community. While I would point out that both sides have had the chance to put their points across in this book, I would have to agree that there is truth in that charge.

Yes, my sympathies lie more with the mothers for the plain and simple fact that these women have no one to turn to, they cannot go public with the accusations that have been made against them and point the finger back at those accusing them. That is wrong. If those making the accusations are so confident, why do they need court orders to stop these issues being made public? There may be nothing to hide, but if people still try to hide information there will always be that suspicion.

Clearly, there has to be a change in the law so that both sides have the same rights – playing on a level pitch, to use an old British saying. As for the question of whether there is such a condition as Munchausen Syndrome by Proxy, I have to say that while I have great respect for the experts who have given their time in this area, I am not convinced, for one main reason. It has been said that the point of MSBP is for someone to gain attention for themselves through harming others. The condition falls down there and then in my eyes. Say, for example, I stab someone or poison their food. When we go to hospital, they will get the attention, not me. If I want attention I will harm myself, I will not harm others.

This is not to say that I do not believe that there are some cases where some people may harm children, but I feel that we are looking at a form of post-natal depression and in nowhere near the numbers that are suggested by social services across the globe.

For children who are being harmed when they are older, I think we are looking at a form of depression, though some people I have spoken to suggest that there may be forms of post-natal depression that affect mothers later on in life as their children grow up. They may have a point. Without further research we cannot be sure.

Again, I have nothing to back this up, but from speaking to both sides and looking at the issue, that is what I think is the problem. I find it ironic that social services are so often involved in so-called MSBP cases. If it is some form of depression, perhaps if the services were more involved beforehand then fewer children would be harmed. But as one social worker said to me when I was writing this book, 'It's a lot harder to claim credit for prevention than it is to cure and save, but it is the proper way'. If this is the attitude of many in the 'caring services' then the services don't need to be reformed, but to be completely rebuilt.

I also think that a lot of the cases of so-called MSBP are nothing more than lazy categorising by overworked and under-resourced social services and medical staff. It is a condition that is very broad in definition and as such works for a number of cases, when in fact the sufferers may have other problems.

One thing that is a real problem though is apathy. Apathy is probably the biggest enemy there is. Many people tend to shy away from getting involved in awkward situations like MSBP accusations. If people get involved and debate the issues, then it has to be discussed, solutions have to be found. It is no use saying that it is something that will never affect you. You don't know that.

However, the above is just my opinion. I would be disappointed if you agreed with every word here and hope you have managed to come to your own conclusions. A resources section overleaf provides more information for those looking for it and many of the works make for interesting reading.

Thank you for your time.

Craig McGill
Scotland

Resources

Books, articles and Web sites that were referenced during the writing of this book. Most of these are presented in easy-to-understand terms for the layperson and are suggested for anyone looking for more details about MSBP or for people – pro- and anti-MSBP – to contact.

Books

Allison, D and Roberts, M (1998) *Disordered Mother or Disordered Diagnosis? Munchausen by Proxy Syndrome*, Analytic Press, London

Schreir, H A and Libow, J (1993) *Hurting for Love*, Guildford Press, New York

Articles

Divasto, P and Saxon, G (1992) 'MSBP in law enforcement', *FBI Law Enforcement Bulletin*, April

Libow, J (1995) 'MSBP victims in adulthood', *Child Abuse and Neglect* (19)

Meadow, R (1977) 'The hinterland of child abuse', *The Lancet*, 13 August

Meadow, R (1995) 'Management of MSBP', *Medico-Legal Journal*, **63**

Morgan, B, 'A study in secrecy', http://www.msbp.com/secrecy.htm

Morley, C J (1995) 'Practical concerns about the diagnosis of MSBP', *Archives of Disease in Childhood* (72)

Web sites

For those unable to go through all the sites here, the first two provide arguments for both sides and comprehensive links/articles.

http://www.ashermeadow.com/
Thoroughly comprehensive MSBP education site and a perfect counterbalance to the next site.

http://www.msbp.com/
Mothers Against Munchausen Syndrome by Proxy Allegations (MAMA).

Other sites

http://www.mindspring.com/~louisalasher/
Louisa Lasher's Factitious Disorder by Proxy/Munchausen Syndrome by Proxy site. (Lasher is a child abuse professional who is devoted full time to MSBP work.)

http://ourworld.compuserve.com/homepages/Marc_Feldman_2/
Dr Marc Feldman's Munchausen Syndrome, Factitious Disorder & Munchausen by Proxy site.

http://mbpeducate.co.uk/

http://www.mbpsnetwork.com/

http://www.medicine.uiowa.edu/pa/sresrch/Huynh/Huynh/sld001.htm
A slide presentation on MSBP.

http://www.yvonneeldridge.org/
Real-life MSBP story.

http://www.medicinenet.com

http://home.rica.net/rthoma/msbp.html
Memos and letters involving those accused of MSBP and those
who diagnose MSBP.

http://www.pnc.com.au/~heleneli/abuse.htm
Helen Hayward-Brown's excellent article on MSBP.

http://www.stop-abuse.de/
A non-profit site that links child advocates, organisations, abuse
victims and others.

http://www.ualberta.ca/~di/csh/bulletin/BulJan00.htm
An online update with Allison and Roberts on their book
Disordered Mother or Disordered Diagnosis? Recommended.

Other

Publications that were useful in researching this book:

The *British Medical Journal*, the *Daily Record*, the *Guardian*, the
Herald, the *Independent*, *LA Daily Journal*, *The Lancet*, *Miami Herald*,
the *Mirror*, *New England Journal of Medicine*, *The New York Times*,
Pittsburgh Post, *Pittsburgh-Post Gazette*, the *Scotsman*, *Staffordshire
Sentinel*, the *Sun*, *Sun-Sentinel Chronicles*, the *Sunday Mirror*,
Sunderland Echo, the *Telegraph*, *UK Press Gazette*, *USA Today* and
The Washington Post.

Index

About the Author

Born in Glasgow in 1973, Craig McGill is an experienced news, sports and features writer. His articles have appeared in many newspapers, magazines and Internet sites, including *Time*, the *Guardian*, the *Sun*, the *Daily Express*, the *Mirror* and the *Scotsman*, with his work having been translated into Norwegian, French and Italian, among other languages.

He is the author of *Football Inc.*, also published by Vision Paperbacks. Future work includes a book on the murder of Asian Scot Surjit Chhokar, and novels.

Currently based in Glasgow, Scotland, Craig can be contacted at the following address: mcgillcraig@hotmail.com.